Dedication

To Nancy Marion Melville DOUGLASS, (1914-1991), a local historian who set herself high standards and whose extensive and meticulous research into the history of the Blue Mountains will benefit future historians.

Pictorial Memories
BLUE MOUNTAINS

John Low

KINGSCLEAR BOOKS

© Kingsclear Books
ABN 99 001 904 034
kingsclear@wr.com.au
www.kingsclearbooks.com.au
PO Box 335 Alexandria 1435

Phone (02) 9439 5093 Facsimile (02) 9439 0430

© Copyright 1991 Kingsclear Books

ISBN 0 908272 37 5

Printed in Australia by McPherson's Printing Group, Maryborough, Victoria

Acknowledgements

The author wishes to express his thanks to the following:

To Alan Sharpe and Catherine Warne of Atrand Pty Ltd who proposed the idea for the book. To Catherine Warne and Lyndon Cummings for the expertise and plain hard work which have seen it through to publication. To Colin Slade, Gwen Silvey, Michael Sharkey and Kerry Leves who contributed sections to the book on their special areas of interest.

To the Macleay Museum, Sydney University, National Library of Australia, Canberra, Mitchell Library, Sydney, Blue Mountains City Library, Blue Mountains Historical Society, Springwood Historical Society, Mount Victoria & District Historical Society, and to all the individuals acknowledged throughout the book from whose personal collections photographs were obtained for use.

To Michael Dark for permission to quote at length from Eleanor Dark's novel *The Little Company*. To Gwen Silvey, Ebena Isles and Helen Halliwell for advice and assistance in finding information and photographs.

To those people whose reminiscences, contributed originally to the Blue Mountains City Library's Oral History Collection, have been used in the writing of this book.

To my wife and children for enduring my absences on so many weekends.

Preface

A popular 1880s tourist guide claimed Sydney had two great attractions — the Harbour and the Mountains. For more than a hundred years the Blue Mountains' cliffs, spectacular waterfalls, mist-filled valleys, romantic hotels and guesthouses, have provided Sydneysiders with a grand retreat.

The Blue Mountains is a region rich in history, a region of rugged terrain, an invigorating climate and dramatic scenery. Diverse impressions are recollected in this book: the presence of Aboriginal tribes; the excited shouts of explorers glimpsing the pastoral potential of the west; the ring of pick and spade on stone; the clanking of chains and the shouted obscenities of bullock drivers; the muffled roar and distant whistle of trains climbing the steep Mountain line; the rural peace of gracious country homes and hotels; invigorating childhood holidays spent in clean Mountain air; the secrets of winding bush tracks; warm nights in cosy guesthouses; spring days in exotic gardens.

A great variety of people have contributed to the Blue Mountains' story. It is hoped that this book will reveal, in both words and pictures, something of the history of this remarkable area and perhaps lead the reader to seek his or her own experience of the marvellous Blue Mountains.

Contents

Why are the Blue Mountains Blue?

While holidaying in Sydney in 1900, Lady Audrey Tennyson, wife of the South Australian Governor, travelled over the Blue Mountains to visit Jenolan Caves. In a long letter written to her mother on her return to Adelaide, she recounted her experiences. Describing the return journey to Katoomba, where she and her husband spent the night at the "very comfortable tho' so cold" Carrington hotel, she remarked on a phenomenon that has impressed and puzzled many visitors to the mountains:

> The afternoon & evening were most beautiful & most wonderful lights & shadows. What struck us more than anything was the wonderfully brilliant blue of the distant hills. I have never seen anything to compare to it at all, the most gorgeous real sapphire blue, really transparent blue— it is impossible to give any idea of it. We wondered whether it was the effect of the gums, & our driver told us it used to be thought so but is an exploded idea, & he agreed with me it must be something in the atmosphere. I shall never forget it.

The blue haze that characterises the mountains had been noted very early. During the first year of the colony's existence Governor Phillip had given the western mountains the names Carmarthen and Lansdowne. In popular conversation, however, these titles were soon abandoned, official declaration being insufficient to prevent the Mountains from being, as Judge-Advocate Collins observed, "commonly known in the colony by the name of the Blue Mountains."

What causes this blueness, the depth and intensity of which is often quite remarkable? In 1955 the Town Clerk of the City of Blue Mountains, tired of being asked this question and being unable to give an assured answer, sought an explanation from the Department of Physics at the University of Sydney. The Head of the Department at the time, Professor Harry Messel, replied in the following terms:

> It is quite certain that the haze which appears to surround any distant object is due to an optical phenomenon called 'Rayleigh scattering'. This effect which was first investigated theoretically by Lord Rayleigh causes the rays of light which impinge on small particles to be scattered in various directions ... Since the atmosphere is always laden with small dust particles, water droplets and the like and since even the air molecules themselves contributed to some extent to the scattering ... if an observer looks at a distant object with the intervening atmosphere illuminated by sunlight, his eyes will receive the blue scattered rays of sunlight in addition to the rays reflected from the object itself. Therefore any distant object will always appear to display some shade of blue.

Professor Messel went on to explain that light is scattered most effectively off very small droplets of oil. He argued that the most plausible explanation of why the Blue Mountains are blue is to be found in the vegetation of the region. Fine oil droplets are dispersed into the atmosphere from such indigenous oil bearing trees as the eucalypts.

It would seem that the puzzled Lady Audrey Tennyson was right on track in her thinking but despite the advances of science no complete answer can be given. In 1955 Professor Messel qualified his explanation with a word of caution at the end of his letter. "I must emphasise that this is merely a guess and that this possibility has to my knowledge not been investigated." In 1991 this would still seem to be the case.

An Ancient Presence

Long before the *Sirius* sailed into Sydney Cove the Blue Mountains knew the presence of humans. When climatic conditions allowed, the abundant water, flora and fauna of the Mountains provided an environment particularly suited to a hunter-gatherer society. Archaeological research has established an Aboriginal presence in the region that is now thought to have begun nearly 22,000 years ago. While the lower slopes of the Mountains seem to have been occupied fairly continuously, there are sites at places like Leura and Blackheath which reveal periods of permanent habitation even in the higher, less climatically kind regions.

All over the Blue Mountains the Aborigines have left their traces. Tool-making sites, rock engravings, and hand stencils in particular, reveal the physical and spiritual presence of a long occupation. To stumble across a cave or rock overhang adorned with a collection of stencils, delicate expressions of an ancient culture, is moving. Surrounded by the sounds and smells of the bush there is the strong feeling of being at the heart of a profound mystery.

For the early European colonists the mystery was great. It confronted them and they did not know what to make of it. Aboriginal culture perplexed them and disturbed their preconceptions of morality and aesthetics. Expressing the general response, Governor Phillip recorded his bafflement that even such a rudimentary pursuit of the arts as he perceived should be practised by a people who showed little inclination to clothe themselves. To his mind it ran contrary to any accepted theory of civilisation. The Aborigines remained incomprehensible and their decline in the Sydney region, which included the Blue Mountains, was swift and brutal.

The geographic area we know as the Blue Mountains was the territory of two tribes. The Gundungurra occupied the Burragorang Valley and the rugged gorges of the southern Blue Mountains, while the Dharug inhabited the northerly regions which included the main ridge.

Pellion's fine portraits of Hara-o and Karadra. (Blue Mts City Lib.)

When Francis Barrallier's expedition penetrated west of Nattai in 1802 he made the first major European contact with the Gundungurras. Barrallier was as perplexed by the Aborigines as any of his fellow Europeans at the time but showed a keen interest in the details of their culture, recording his observations in a journal about domestic and group relations, placenames, native foods, weapons and other artefacts. His description of a boomerang, for example, is indicative of his genuine curiosity about Aboriginal life:

> The natives of this part of the country make use of a weapon which is not employed, and is even unknown to, the natives of Sydney. It is composed of a piece of wood in the form of a half circle, which they make as sharp as a sabre on both edges, and pointed at each end. They throw it on the ground or in the air, making it revolve on itself, and with such a velocity that one cannot see it returning towards the ground; only the whizzing of it is heard. When they throw it along the ground it is exactly like a cannon-ball, knocking down everything on its passage.

Such accounts of traditional Gundungurra life add a dimension of interest and value to his journal not found in the accounts of other Blue Mountains' explorers.

Seventeen years after Barrallier's adventures in the southern Blue Mountains, three members of a

French scientific expedition visiting Sydney in 1819 crossed the Blue Mountains on their way to Bathurst. Their journey over the recently discovered route to the West lay in Dharug territory and the account of their trip offers rare insight into early Aboriginal-European relations on the Blue Mountains, an area that has generally gone unrecorded.

At Springwood, near the military depot where they spent the night, Quoy, Gaudichaud and Pellion came upon an Aboriginal camp. In a small hut built with the flattened bark of some eucalyptus trees, they found a young Aboriginal tending to the needs of a sick old man. Their guide "recognised this old man as Karadra, supreme chief or king of that part of the mountain. No one, according to him, had proved more dangerous to the English, many of whom had perished at his hand, without anyone ever being able to catch him in the act. For a long time, however, this man had been peacefully disposed towards the settlers; ... We asked the younger of these natives to fetch us a gourd of water, which he at once did; we then left them after making them several presents." (G. Mackaness).

The account highlights the Aboriginal opposition to European encroachment on their territory. Disease may have been the principal killer but bloodshed was also present. Karadra was a skilled guerilla leader and not averse to allying himself with the whites against the depredations of his own enemies.

J. T. Ryan, an early pioneer of the Penrith district, recalls in his *Reminiscences of Australia* the terrible retribution incited by Aboriginal acts of resistance. Some years before the French scientists passed through Springwood, the military depot had been attacked and a soldier killed. A band of vigilantes from the Windsor-Nepean district went in pursuit. They took the Aborigines by surprise in the mountains south of the Grose River and slaughtered the men, women and children.

A European Perspective

In June 1789 Governor Phillip and his companions arrived at the conjunction of the Hawkesbury and Grose Rivers. The roar of the Grose, as it rushed out of the Mountains, was deafening and the abundant flood wreckage littering the river flats was an indication of its power. This was a portent of the dangerous and enigmatic landscape that awaited the first explorers to venture into these 'hills' that showed so softly blue on the horizon.

Despite the uncertain hold the colonists had on this strange, inhospitable land, their European faith in Man's mastery over the rest of the natural world gave them little reason to doubt that the mysteries of what lay beyond these mountains would soon be made clear.

This was not to be. With their innocently English names of Carmarthen, Richmond and Lansdowne, these blue mountains were soon to prove remarkably unEnglish in character and for the next twenty years would define the limits of the colony's westward expansion. The cryptic terrain defied and frustrated every attempt at penetration, and the early optimism

Artist Alphonse Pellion drew Aborigines from the Nepean and Springwood. Aurang-Jack, "a chief of Springwood" and his two wives (bottom) provide us with the earliest precise detail of the appearance of Blue Mountains full-blood Aborigines. (Blue Mts City Lib.)

of Phillip's hastily uttered intention "shortly to explore their summits" soon collapsed.

The first expedition to venture west of the Nepean set the pattern of frustration. In December 1789 the marine lieutenant William Dawes encountered a "succession of deep ravines, the sides of which were frequently inaccessible" and reached a point slightly north-east of present-day Linden. Here, as far as the eye could see, the country was merely a repetition of that which his party had just traversed with such difficulty.

A succession of explorers followed, driven on by the need for geographical knowledge vital to the survival of the infant colony, the pursuit of scientific data and the sheer spirit of adventure. William Paterson (1793), Matthew Everingham (1795) and George Caley (1804) all explored the northern regions of the Mountains while expeditions led by George Bass (1796), John Wilson (1798) and Francis Barrallier (1802) tackled the wilderness to the south-west.

By 1805 optimism had deteriorated. Governor King's resigned judgment was that any further attempt to cross the Mountains would be "as chimerical as useless" and that "As far as respects the extension of agriculture beyond the first range of mountains, that is an idea that must be given up."

Lachlan Macquarie established himself in office on the first of January 1810. The population of the colony had grown and farms and stock had spread. Gregory Blaxland was one of an emerging class of 'gentlemen farmers' who concentrated on what Macquarie cynically referred to as "the lazy object of rearing cattle". Blaxland was among those affected by the shortage of available land. As he looked toward the blue smudge in the west from his South Creek farm, Blaxland saw the solution lay in finding a way over those mountains. Between 1810 and 1813 he made two reconnaissance expeditions along their periphery, confirming "the opinion that it was practicable to find a passage over the mountains." He would launch his attack "by the ridge which

appeared to run westward between the Warragomby and the River Grose."

Blaxland approached two others to accompany him in his venture. The first was William Lawson, an ensign in the N.S.W. Corps who had embarked upon an agricultural career that would eventually see him become one of the largest landholders west of the Mountains. The second was the young William Charles Wentworth, born on a convict ship bound for Norfolk Island in 1790. His star was destined to rise meteorically on the colonial scene. He had just taken up a large grant of land on the Nepean and was purchasing cattle from the Government stock.

On 11 May 1813 the "dauntless three" (as Henry Kendall described them) departed with their four servants, five dogs and four horses to do battle "with the haughty heights". Testimony to the correctness of Blaxland's judgement is the route they traversed which is still the one used by travellers today.

Standing on the high point at Mount Blaxland, at the termination of their forward journey, with Canaan stretching away before them, Blaxland remarked that the country they were now looking at was "sufficient in extent ... to support the stock of the Colony for the next thirty years". The 1813 journey opened the way for the development in the west of a powerful pastoral industry which would exert a profound influence upon the social, political and economic development of New South Wales during the nineteenth century. Its impact upon traditional Aboriginal society in the west would be devastating.

In November Macquarie despatched Surveyor George Evans to establish beyond doubt the existence of these valuable lands in the west. Evans and his five companions surveyed their predecessors' route and reached Mount Blaxland in eight days. They then travelled another 160 kilometres further than Blaxland, Lawson and Wentworth, returning in early January 1814.

The newly discovered western lands could be of no economic value until they were linked to the eastern seaboard by the construction of a road over

A young Gregory Blaxland drawn around the time he made the crossing. (Mitchell Lib.)

the Blue Mountains. In his journal, William Lawson had commented that there would be "no difficulty in making a good road to it" and, to achieve this end, Macquarie agreed to the appointment, in July 1814, of William Cox as Superintendent of the project. He was the then Chief Magistrate at Windsor. Six months later, in the heat of January 1815, a road suitable for animal and cart transport was completed to the site of present-day Bathurst.

The Explorers' Tree

Australians are familiar with the story of Blaxland, Lawson and Wentworth. Their journey has become part of the nation's folklore and 'The Explorers' Tree' situated just west of Katoomba, on the rise known as

"The Explorers Marked Tree" n.d.
(Blue Mts City Lib.)

Pulpit Hill, is one of the well-known Blue Mountains' symbols.

There is some uncertainty as to when the tree first came to public notice. The record of what was actually cut into its trunk has also been thrust into the realm of public debate. This happened, for example, in the letter columns of the *Sydney Morning Herald* in 1905 and again, more recently, in the *Blue Mountains Echo* in 1983 when the local tourist officer argued that the tree had been manufactured as a tourist attraction in the late nineteenth century.

The earliest reference to the marked tree seems to have appeared in a letter written by Rev. William Woolls to the *Sydney Morning Herald* in August,

1867, in which he noted "the blackbutt on which the late Mr W. Lawson cut his initials with a tomahawk in 1813." In the early 1870s Eccleston Du Faur also reported the tree's existence, but referred to it only as "the L tree". By 1884, when a wall and fence were built around the tree (eventually resulting in its death) the plaque attached claimed that it was "Marked by Blaxland, Lawson and Wentworth". In 1905 the current tourist guidebook stated that the tree bore the initials "W B above and L below the W". To confuse matters further, this guidebook also pointed out that numerous other letter carvings were also on the tree.

Considering the inconsistency of the record and the fact that after the Western Road was opened in 1815, Pulpit Hill became a favoured resting place for

travellers and stock, perhaps the 'Explorers' Tree' is a true creation of the 'folk'.

Whatever the historical truth, the tree's validity as a popular icon is unquestioned. It remains a symbolic link with the early period of exploration, a period for which there are few tangible remnants in the Blue Mountains.

"The dauntless three! For twenty days and nights
These heroes battled with the haughty heights
For twenty spaces of the stars and sun
These Romans kept their harness buckled on!"
Henry Kendall, on 25 December 1880.
(Sydney Mail, Mitchell Lib.)

"With pick and spade"

When "the dauntless three" stood on the high point now known as Mount Blaxland and reflected upon the forested landscape stretching away before them, they were confident in the words of William Lawson that there would be "no difficulty in making a road to it." For the newly discovered western pastures to be of any economic value to the colony it was essential to link them to the eastern seaboard.

In November 1813, Surveyor George Evans was despatched by Governor Lachlan Macquarie to confirm the account of the expedition. By the end of July 1814, William Cox, former Chief Magistrate at Windsor, was on the Mountains superintending a road using a plot of Evan's traverse as his guide. He had been instructed by Macquarie to build a road "at least 12 feet wide, so as to permit two carts or other wheeled carriages to pass each other with ease."

Using only very basic methods and tools, his convict workmen completed the road as far as Bathurst by mid-January 1815. This was a considerable achievement despite the extremely primitive result. At many points along the route the terrain had posed Cox numerous problems, some of which continued to trouble travellers and surveyors for many years. It would be some time before a permanent line was established.

In the following decades surveyors plotted and measured improvements. In the early 1820s William Lawson pioneered alternatives to both the eastern (now the Old Bathurst Road) and the western (Lawson's Long Alley) ascents of the Blue Mountains.

In 1823, James McBrien re-surveyed the line of the Western Road and a new route to the west via Kurrajong was discovered by nineteen-year-old Archibald Bell and surveyed by Robert Hoddle.

The most substantial improvements to the road undoubtedly occurred under the Surveyor-Generalship of Major Thomas Mitchell who succeeded to this office on the death of John Oxley in 1828. In Mitchell's view public works like roads and bridges were the principal indicators by which one measured the progress of civilization. In the late 1820s and early 1830s he spent considerable time surveying and marking out the colony's system of main roads and effecting permanent improvements.

One of the principal responsibilities of the colonial government in the first half of the nineteenth century was to use convict labour efficiently. The construction and maintenance of roads and other public works occupied large numbers of convicts and the convict road gang became a common sight for travellers across the Blue Mountains.

This was the very hardest of hard labour a convict could expect to experience, especially if his record of misdemeanours led him to be assigned to an iron gang. Here he would be expected to work in shackles, "bound down with iron chains."

The convict road gangs were under guard at all times and subject to strict discipline. They were housed in temporary accommodation such as that observed by the Quaker, James Backhouse, in 1835: "moveable caravans, which have doors, and iron-barred windows, on one side."

There were also more permanent convict 'communities' dotted along the Western Road. 'Stockades', for example, existed at Emu Plains, Twenty Mile Hollow (Bull's Camp at Linden), Blackheath and Hartley. In 1846 Lt. Colonel Godfrey Charles Mundy was travelling to Bathurst and described the stockade at Blackheath which had been transferred from Twenty Mile Hollow two years earlier. It was a melancholy scene.

The barracks and convict "boxes" form a little hamlet of some two dozen buildings of white-washed slabs with tall stone chimneys, laid out on a rocky plateau cleared of trees, and commanding a prospect of melancholy and desolate sterility ... The prisoners here form what is called an iron-gang — or ironed gang. They are employed working, in chains, and for periods according to sentence, on the repairs of the high road. We passed several lots of these wretched creatures — England's galley-slaves — clanking along with straddling-gait and hopeless hang-dog looks to their allotted labours, escorted by soldiers; or working with pick and spade, crowbar, maule and wedge on the stubborn rocks — working with mule-like slowness and sulkiness forced to work by fear of the lash.

A Master Mason

In 1831 Mitchell was asked by Governor Darling to design plans for the proposed town of Emu at the foot of the Blue Mountains. Again, the Surveyor-General found his views at variance with those in authority.

Lawson's zig zag alternative to Cox's original route up Lapstone Hill was proving inadequate. Its steep, sharp curves and instability in wet weather were resulting in numerous complaints from travellers and the Governor recommended the stationing of a permanent repair gang on the Hill.

This smacked of a short-term solution and Mitchell was unimpressed. He examined the area himself and suggested a new route that would follow the gully of Lapstone Creek and join the existing road near the Pilgrim Inn. He argues that the problem of the Western Road up Lapstone Hill had to be addressed and a permanent line established before any thought could be given to building a town on Emu Plains.

This time his advice was accepted and work began on the new pass in August 1832. During the course of construction half way up the proposed pass, it was found that a bridge was needed to cross the creek. Mitchell rejected the flimsy wooden structures in current use throughout the colony. Easy victims of flood and fire, they were not compatible with his vision of permanent settlement. What was required was a solidly built stone bridge, a model for future major roads.

Only one stone bridge, at Richmond in Tasmania, had previously been built in Australia and artisans equipped with the technical knowledge and experience relevant to their construction were

Augustus Earle's "View from the Summit of Mt York, looking towards the Bathurst Plains, convicts breaking stones" ca. 1826 (Nan Kivell Collection, National Lib.)

virtually unknown. It was a remarkable coincidence which solved Mitchell's problem. In the same month work began on the pass at Emu a master mason of twenty year's experience arrived in Sydney.

David Lennox had worked on a number of major bridge projects in Britain. When Mitchell made his acquaintance, Lennox was employed as a day labourer building the stone wall outside the Legislative Council Chambers in Macquarie Street. His talents were re-directed immediately.

Mitchell enjoyed telling the story of the amazing circumstances of his discovery and the speed with which he appointed Lennox, describing how the latter "left his stone wall and with his shirt sleeves still tucked up — and trowel in hand — undertook to plan stone bridges for this colony".

From late 1832 until mid-1833 Lennox worked with a group of about twenty convicts selected personally from the larger road gang. He was, according to Assistant Surveyor John Abbott, "indefatigable in instructing them how to work" and a good relationship appears to have developed. A number went with him to his next assignment at Prospect Creek on the Great Southern Road near Liverpool.

The bridge, with its gently sweeping 'horseshoe' curve, was completed in early July 1833. It was the first of an impressive list of achievements by David Lennox. Described by Mitchell as "a somewhat

Charles Rodius' "Convicts building the road to Bathurst over the Blue Mountains" in 1833, at Mitchell's Pass. (National Library)

Surveyor-General Mitchell, (Mitchell Library)

experimental work", Lennox Bridge at Lapstone is testimony of Mitchell's commitment to enduring public works. It formed part of the main route to the west for almost a hundred years and carried traffic the like of which the Surveyor-General and his Superintendent of Bridges could not have dreamed possible.

Worthy of any line of road in England

In 1830, following Governor Darling's request that Surveyor-General Mitchell determine an improved line to Bathurst with "as little delay as possible", the surveyor turned his talents to the Western Road.

In the 1880s, Lennox's bridge was used as the common thoroughfare for mountain traffic. Today it stands off the Great Western Highway nestled in the bush near the Lapstone Incline. (Mitchell Library)

During the course of his survey he marked "a very favourable descent from the Blue Mountains, by a ridge nearly parallel to that of Mount York, but more in a direct line". He named the ridge Mount Victoria.

At this time work was already in progress on a new descent of the western escarpment, begun a year or two earlier under the supervision of Major E. Lockyer. The fact that this alternative route, situated

between the original Cox's Road and Lawson's Long Alley, had received official sanction and was well advanced did not deter Mitchell. He moved the work gangs over to Mount Victoria, convinced that his

Since 1832 Victoria Pass has remained the principal route of access to the West thanks to Mitchell's judgement and determination. (Blue Mts City Lib.)

decision was correct and the line marked could not be bettered.

When the Colonial Secretary, Alexander McLeay, was notified, Mitchell was firmly reprimanded and instructed to cease work on the new pass immediately. Had Mitchell been a less determined personality things may have ended there and Lockyer's road been completed but Mitchell was not about to give up.

His diary records that he was "much vexed" and sat up late into the evening composing a reply. He ordered his men to continue with "vigorous activity" and responded in the following terms:

> I defy any man to point out any material improvements in the lines laid down by me ... The Secretary of State has been pleased to place the Road Department under my directions; and although the addition to my duties makes no addition in my salary, I cannot conscientiously sit down in Sydney and pocket that salary without caring whether roads be made right or wrong ... and I trust that the work I have begun, on no vague report of any illiterate clown, but after a general survey by myself and assistants, may be suffered to proceed ...

After a further refusal to sanction his work the dispute laboured on until September, 1830, when Mitchell demanded his case be put in London. An interview with the Governor finally resolved matters and Mitchell won grudging approval for work to continue.

In February 1832, nearly four hundred convicts were working on the Pass and its spectacular stone causeways or 'bridges'. By October it was ready to carry traffic and was opened on the 23rd by Governor Bourke.

The Pass of Victoria was much praised by later travellers. Charles Darwin called it "worthy of any line of road in England". For a brief period between 1912 and 1920 early automobiles preferred the easier grades of Berghofer's Pass. Otherwise, Victoria Pass has remained the principal route of access to the west. What greater vindication of his judgement could Mitchell have hoped for?

A stream of gold diggers ascend the Lapstone incline where "the roads are so cut up that ruts often cover the axletrees and breakdowns are met on every steep pass." Illustrated London News, 15 November 1851. (Blue Mts City Lib.)

"A tolerable night's rest"

In 1815 the opening of Cox's Road was an occasion of some ceremony. Before winter set in, Governor Macquarie, his wife and a large entourage travelled over the new road, camping at several spots on the Mountains and proclaiming the site of Bathurst.

Travel in the early years was closely regulated by the Government. "Gentlemen or other respectable free persons" desiring permission to travel over the Mountains were required to make written application and were issued with a special pass if approved.

To ensure the enforcement of this regulation a military depot was established in 1815 on the site of one of Cox's supply stores near what is now Glenbrook Lagoon. The following year the depot was moved to Springwood, named by Macquarie for its "pretty wooded plain near a spring of very good fresh water". It remained here until the mid-1840s.

Although controls on travel to the West were gradually eased, settlement on the Blue Mountains remained negligible until the advent of the railway. The road provided a link between the coast and the inland and transformed the Mountains from a barrier into a key element in the colony's development.

Travel over the Mountains, particularly in the early years, was difficult and often dangerous. The road was rough and often eroded, and took a heavy toll on vehicles. At some points in wet weather it was virtually impassable. It followed its lonely and tortuous route along a narrow ridge top. On either side was the unexplored bush, forbidding and alien to minds still rooted in European traditions. The Blue Mountains was not a place one wished to be in for too long.

In 1822, in a letter to her sister in England, Mrs Elizabeth Hawkins wrote a dramatic account of her family's trip to Bathurst where her husband, Thomas, was to take up an appointment as commissariat storekeeper. With her eight children and her elderly mother to care for, it was an arduous and uncomfortable eighteen days she spent on the road.

You must understand that the whole of the road from beginning to the end of the mountains is cut entirely through a forest, nor can you go in a direct line to Bathurst from one mountain to another, but you are obliged often to wind round the edges of them, and at times to look down such precipices as would make you shudder. We ascended. Our cart had now three bullocks, as we had so much trouble to get on with two, but we were worse off than ever. As the ascent became worse they refused to drag, and every few minutes first one and then another would lie down. The dogs were summoned to bark at them and bit their noses to make them get up. The barking of the dogs, the bellowing of the bullocks and the swearing of the men made our heads ache, and kept us in continual terror. That was exactly the case every day of the journey.

To Barron Field, Judge of the Supreme Court of N.S.W. and traveller to Bathurst in the same year as Mrs Hawkins, the Blue Mountains were "thrown together in a monotonous manner" and clothed in "a mere sea of harsh trees". The King's Tableland, he found "anarchical and untabular as any His Majesty possesses", while Blackheath, named by Macquarie in 1815, was "a wretched misnomer. Not to mention its awful contrast to that beautiful place of that name in England, heath it is none. Black it may be when the shrubs are burnt, as they often are." Arrival at Mount York was a relief "for it leads you to the first green valley."

Later visitors such as Charles Darwin (1836) and Louisa Meredith (1839) were also disappointed. Darwin was impressed and inspired by the Weatherboard Falls and Govett's Leap but for the rest he found the scenery "exceedingly monotonous". Meredith's account reflected upon "a wild and barren country" characterised by "monotony" and "deformity" and filled with "trees without foliage, hills and valleys alike destitute of verdure". The contemplation of it oppressed her and she passed the time dreaming "of the green and beautiful plains of Bathurst" promised at the end of her journey.

For most travellers, the journey over the Blue

"We then halted at three o'clock in a very pretty wooded plain near a spring of very good fresh water, and pitched our tent near the side of the road," wrote Governor Lachlan Macquarie in 1815. John Lewin, the painter of "Springwood" was part of the entourage (Mitchell Library)

Mountains was no fun and required them to dig deep into their reserves of endurance. The only semblance of civilization to be found in this remote and lonely place was that afforded by the inns that started to appear at strategic points along the road from the middle of the 1820s. Following the establishment of Collit's Inn at the foot of Mount York in 1823, the number of these accommodation houses increased as travel restrictions were lifted and the flow of people to the west accelerated.

In the decade following the discovery of payable gold at Ophir in 1851, traffic along the Western Road became heavier than at any other times since its construction. When William Derrincourt went to the diggings in the 1850s, he found that the road over the Blue Mountains "resembled a well-used ant track". He encountered all manner of travellers, "from the wheelbarrow trundler with goods and chattels, to the

common pedestrian with pick and shovel, tin dish, and blanket swag on back, and here and there a man and wife loaded to the utmost with necessaries for the venture, some of the children, and in many cases dogs, bearing their share of the burden".

Inn accommodation varied from the miserable to the comfortable as Louisa Meredith discovered during her journey in 1839. After the steep climb up Lapstone Hill her party "stayed to breakfast at a small wayside public house, where the slovenly slipshod women, dirty floors, and a powerful odour of stale tobacco-smoke, gave me no very favourable expectations of cleanliness or comfort". On the walls, heavily stained with smoke, hung a number of cheap, brightly coloured prints bearing titles like 'The Faithful Lover' and 'The Bethrothed'.

Outside, the surrounds of "this comfortless habitation" were untidy and neglected, and rubbish

On January 18, 1836 Charles Darwin *"walked about three miles to see Govett's Leap: a view similar but even perhaps more stupendous character than that near the Weatherboard. So early in the day the gulf was filled with a thin blue haze."* The Picturesque Atlas of Australasia. *(Blue Mts City Lib.)*

was strewn around and between the "wretchedly dilapidated outhouses and stables" a strong smell pervaded the whole scene which was appropriately completed by a number of dirty children "lounging about in close companionship with the pigs ... but apparently less lively".

It is not certain which inn Mrs Meredith was describing but The Pilgrim and The Lord Byron at the top of Lapstone Hill and The Woolpack at The Valley (Heights) are possible candidates.

Later in her journey Louisa Meredith sampled the fare at "Blind Paddy's", The Shepherd and His Flock Inn, at Pulpit Hill. Here her experience was somewhat better, the hosts being "a couple of decent elderly women" who welcomed the party "into a small but clean whitewashed room, gaily adorned with feathers, shells, and the droll little pictures usually found in such houses".

After a repast "by no means contemptible" and warmed by "a bright wood-fire", she enjoyed "a tolerable night's rest" in a room no bigger than a ship's cabin but containing "a clean dimity bed and window curtains". The next morning found her "quite recruited and ready for setting forth again on our onward journey".

When the railway was laid across the Blue Mountains in the late 1860s the wayside inns lost their patronage as traffic along the road declined. Proprietors moved on and many of the old inns were sold, some being transformed into private residences, others refurbished as hotels and guesthouses. Most, in the course of time, have disappeared altogether.

The Pilgrim Inn

Occupying a key position at the intersection of alternative routes up the eastern escarpment, this inn was built in the late 1820s and received its first licence in 1830. It was operated by James Evans whose son Edwin later played cricket for Australia. In the late 1830s a second inn, The Lord Byron, was established

Built in the 1820s, the Pilgrim Inn at Blaxland was destroyed by bushfire in 1968. (Blue Mts City Lib.)

nearby. This has led to considerable confusion for, during the 1850s and 1860s, John Outrim Wascoe owned both licences and used the sign of The Pilgrim interchangeably. The original inn was sold at auction in 1860 and became a private residence for the next hundred years. It was destroyed by bushfire in 1968. The Lord Byron had been demolished half a century earlier, in 1912.

In 1865 an incident occurred at The Pilgrim Inn (or was it The Lord Byron?) which gave Wascoe's establishment a more than local notoriety. Sir Frederick Pottinger, the much maligned Police Inspector for western N.S.W., was on his way to Sydney to seek redress for his recent dismissal over a breach of police regulations. On 5 March his coach made a refreshment stop at Wascoe's and, in his haste to rejoin the vehicle on its departure, Sir Frederick's pistol accidentally discharged, inflicting a wound that eventually proved fatal. The man who had harassed Ben Hall throughout the western district died in Sydney a month later, on 9 April.

The Woolpack

The Woolpack was the first inn in the Springwood district and was opened in 1831 as The Valley Inn, on land opposite the present Valley Heights Railway Station. The name changed four years later. In 1835 the Quaker, James Backhouse, recorded in his

journal that "on reaching a place, called The Valley, where there is a plain, country inn, with the sign of The Woolpack, having moderate accommodation, we gladly rested for the night."

When Governor Fitzroy and his cousin, Colonel Mundy, passed the establishment in 1846 it had undergone a further name change. It was now The Welcome Inn, operated "by a jolly old soldier named James, who rejoices in a Waterloo medal, a pretty daughter and what is more to our purpose than either, some excellent bottled ale."

Following the arrival of the railway, the inn was purchased by the Hon. Geoffrey Eagar who converted it into a country home and renamed it Wyoming. When Eagar died, it operated for many years as a guesthouse and was eventually demolished in 1937.

The Woolpack ca. 1930s. (Springwood Historical Society)

The Scotch Thistle, Blackheath

In July, 1831, the Scotch Thistle, a low stone building with shingle roof, opened in Blackheath. Its landlord, Andrew Gardner, was an ex-convict who had prospered in the 1820s as a farmer and publican on the western slopes of the Divide and now hoped to provide "suitable accommodation for respectable travellers" on the Blue Mountains.

When the young naturalist, Charles Darwin, arrived one warm evening in January 1836, he

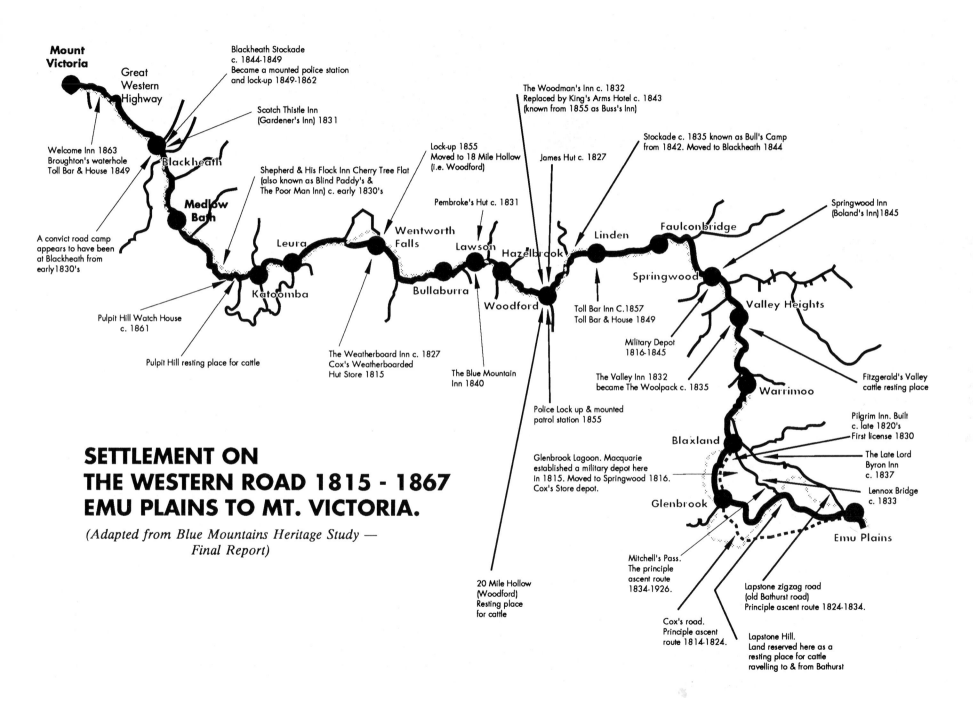

Mount Victoria

Great Western Highway

Blackheath Stockade c. 1844-1849 Became a mounted police station and lock-up 1849-1862

Scotch Thistle Inn (Gardener's Inn) 1831

The Woodman's Inn c. 1832 Replaced by King's Arms Hotel c. 1843 (known from 1855 as Buss's Inn)

Stockade c. 1835 known as Bull's Camp from 1842. Moved to Blackheath 1844

James Hut c. 1827

Welcome Inn 1863 Broughton's waterhole Toll Bar & House 1849

Blackheath

Lock-up 1855 Moved to 18 Mile Hollow (i.e. Woodford)

Springwood Inn (Boland's Inn) 1845

Medlow Bath

Shepherd & His Flock Inn Cherry Tree Flat (also known as Blind Paddy's & The Poor Man Inn) c. early 1830's

Pembroke's Hut c. 1831

Faulconbridge

A convict road camp appears to have been at Blackheath from early 1830's

Wentworth Falls

Linden

Leura

Lawson

Hazelbrook

Springwood

Valley Heights

Katoomba

Bullaburra

Woodford

Pulpit Hill Watch House c. 1861

Toll Bar Inn C.1857 Toll Bar & House 1849

Military Depot 1816-1845

Fitzgerald's Valley cattle resting place

Pulpit Hill resting place for cattle

The Weatherboard Inn c. 1827 Cox's Weatherboarded Hut Store 1815

The Blue Mountain Inn 1840

The Valley Inn 1832 became The Woolpack c. 1835

Warrimoo

Police Lock up & mounted patrol station 1855

Pilgrim Inn. Built c. late 1820's First license 1830

Blaxland

The Late Lord Byron Inn c. 1837

SETTLEMENT ON THE WESTERN ROAD 1815 - 1867 EMU PLAINS TO MT. VICTORIA.

(Adapted from Blue Mountains Heritage Study — Final Report)

Glenbrook Lagoon. Macquarie established a military depot here in 1815. Moved to Springwood 1816. Cox's Store depot.

Glenbrook

Lennox Bridge c. 1833

Emu Plains

Mitchell's Pass. The principle ascent route 1834-1926.

20 Mile Hollow (Woodford) Resting place for cattle

Lapstone zigzag road (old Bathurst road) Principle ascent route 1824-1834.

Cox's road. Principle ascent route 1814-1824.

Lapstone Hill. Land reserved here as a resting place for cattle ravelling to & from Bathurst

remarked on the comfort of the inn and noted its similarity to "the small inns in North Wales".

Inn life was not always comfortable as Sarah Wilson, who ran the inn with her husband during the period 1838 to 1840, recounted to a Sydney journalist in the 1890s: "We never had trouble with the (bush) rangers, but once were robbed by a convict named Ryan, who got into our bedroom, took everything, and threatened to kill my husband. He had a beautiful little dog that did some wonderful tricks, and when he was arrested both the colonel and the sergeant wanted him to give them the dog, but he dashed its brains out on a rock rather than do so." (*Sydney Mail*, 12 December 1896)

When the railway terminated at Mt Victoria in the 1860s, Blackheath went into a temporary decline. For almost a decade the Scotch Thistle appears to have remained unlicensed and even derelict. Its salvation was its proximity to the grandeur of Govett's Leap, a 'sight' that continued to be a highlight in the Blue Mountains.

In 1878 a Sydney businessman with the unusual name of Truth Butts, informed "the Gentry of Sydney and others" that he had opened the Govett's Leap Hotel. The change in name reflected the future of the Blue Mountains. Passing travellers were now being replaced by visitors who came to stay for an extended period, attracted by the region's natural wonders. The inn had become an hotel and the following year its name was altered once again to the exotic Hydora.

Gradually substantial changes were made to the building. A weatherboard extension fronting the main road was added in 1879 and then substantially rebuilt as a double-storeyed brick unit in the early twentieth century. Extended further at the end of World War I and renamed the Astoria, the hotel entered the 1920s "replete with every modern convenience".

The original inn section was finally demolished in 1938 and new additions built on the site, which marked a further change in name — to Gardner's Inn!

The Scotch Thistle opened in Blackheath in 1831, later became the Govett's Leap Hotel, the Hydora, the Astoria, and today — Gardner's Inn. (Blue Mts Hist. Soc.)

The Mount Victoria Inn & John William Berghofer

Situated at the foot of Thomas Mitchell's Victoria Pass, the Mount Victoria Inn was built in 1839 by William Cummings of Bathurst. During the decades prior to the arrival of the railway, the inn served as a regular stop for the coaches that plied the Western Road and as a haven and meeting place for the foot-weary and saddle-sore.

A later visitor, writing in the 1890s, reflected on "the rosy gold-digging days" when the inn prospered as "a coach horse-changing station and great bullock-drivers' camp, where blowing, oaths, and expletives generally were freely scattered about, and old Jamaica swallowed in puncheons." He noted that "extensive stabling accommodation can be seen at the rear of the hotel; also what was once a blacksmith's shop."

The Delaney family, who later became prominent in the commercial life of Mount Victoria and Blackheath, established their butchery business at the inn in the mid-1870s and operated from there until transferring to Mount Victoria sometime in the 1880s. It appears that they also maintained the building's role as a road-side hostelry during this time.

In 1892 the Mount Victoria Inn was bought by John William Berghofer, former manager of the large Kanimbla station in the valley of the same name. He converted the property for use as his private residence and renamed it 'Rosenthal' — Valley of the Roses — the name he remembered from his childhood home in Hessia, Germany.

Berghofer, who had arrived in Australia as a boy in 1855, was a remarkable man whose contribution to public life on the Mountains was substantial. For many years he served as Chairman of the Mount Victoria Progress Association. In 1906, at the age of sixty-three, he was elected the first President of the new Blaxland Shire Council and continued an active involvement in local government affairs until 1916.

In the early years of motoring when cars were

The Mount Victoria Inn at the foot of Victoria Pass in 1887. (Macleay Museum).

finding difficulty with the grades of Victoria Pass, it was due to the efforts of Berghofer that an alternative access on the western escarpment was built and opened in 1912. Berghofer's Pass was preferred by motorists for over a decade until, in the 1920s, the power of motor vehicles improved and Victoria Pass returned to popularity.

A naturalised citizen, Berghofer had always been interested in Australian history and was influential in establishing the Obelisk in memory of Blaxland, Lawson and Wentworth at Mount York in 1900. With the opening of Berghofer's Pass, he devoted himself to organising a Centenary Celebration of the First Crossing of the Blue Mountains. He was indefatigable in his urgings and inspirational in his leadership and later became known as "The Father of the Centenary Movement".

On 28 May, 1913, at the banquet held in Mount Victoria prior to the unveiling of the Memorial Pavilion at Mount York, Berghofer proposed the toast to the early explorers and pioneers. At the end of his speech he was "loudly cheered".

Three years later, the joy of those cheers had soured to bitterness as life in the Blue Mountains was poisoned by anti-German sentiment. Hailed as a great patriot during he celebrations of 1913, Berghofer was disqualified as a councillor in May 1916 and saw his name removed from the Pass he had initiated. The depth of the torment he endured at this time is reflected in his decision to anglicise the name of his family home to 'Rosedale'.

Though the indignities of this period could not be erased, his public reputation was restored once the war was over. In 1927, two months before his death at the age of eighty-seven, he was ceremoniously presented to the Duke and Duchess of York during their visit to the Blue Mountains and Jenolan Caves.

John William Berghofer's position as a pioneer of the district is well-established and the pass that bears his name is now a popular walking track.

Whitton's Mountain Railway

On the morning of 17 June, 1867, a small engine, polished to gleaming in the winter light, rattled west towards the Blue Mountains, pulling the first excursion train. Its destination was Wentworth Falls, then known as The Weatherboard, 867 metres above sea level.

Crossing Emu Plains, the train's passengers were confronted with a memorable sight. Outlined against a dark blue-green background of bush was the sharp white profile of a stone viaduct. From the distance of the plains its series of graceful semi-circular arches,

The Knapsack Viaduct was described by the Illawarra Mercury *on 21 February in 1865 as "... certainly the most imposing, picturesque, finely proportioned, and substantial structure of which New South Wales can boast." (Macleay Museum)*

supported by slender, white, tapering piers was a scene of "exceedingly light and airy appearance ... the whole structure but a picture in stone." (*Illawarra Mercury,* 21 February, 1865) This was an inspiring way to begin the ascent of the Blue Mountains.

The man largely responsible for this was a determined young Yorkshireman, John Whitton. Appointed Engineer-in-Chief of the New South Wales Railways in March 1856, Whitton came to Australia with considerable experience of railway construction in England and a firm faith in the future of a steam powered rail system.

By 1862 the western railway line had been completed to Penrith. In 1857, a survey by the Royal Engineers concluded a further extension to Bathurst was impracticable. In the light of this, a faction led by Governor Denison advocated a system of light horse tramways.

Whitton strenuously opposed this and sent out his own surveyors. He decided that a western rail route was a practical proposition providing it followed the line over the Mountains taken by the road. Submitting a detailed report in 1861 he proposed that "the lines described by me ... be constructed and worked throughout by steam power." The Government was convinced.

The economics of the project were to impose severe restrictions on its application. Tunnels had to be eliminated, the maximum grades increased, tighter curves imposed and railside buildings reduced to a minimum. His imaginative and technical powers were taxed to the limit. With tunnels considered too costly, Whitton decided on a method to raise and lower trains over the mountainous terrain. This method had been successfully employed in both the United States and India. Zig zags would be constructed on both the eastern and western flanks of the Blue Mountains.

Work began on the zig zag and seven-arched viaduct at Lapstone in 1863 and by 1865 it was being hailed as a landmark in Australian engineering. The *Empire* proclaimed the viaduct "the finest piece of masonry in New South Wales" and a tangible indication of "what colonial contractors can do if allowed fair play."

By the middle of 1867 the track had been laid as far as The Weatherboard which became a bustling railway terminus. Here, passengers transferred to coaches to complete their westward journey. A year or so later, in May 1868, Mount Victoria became the terminus while work continued on the descent of the western escarpment. Here the 'Great Zig Zag', with its three large viaducts, tunnel at Clarence, and deep rock cuttings, was being fashioned out of the wilderness.

A traveller, Edmond Marin La Meslee, remarked that: "It seems miraculous that human brains and brawn should have been able to conceive and construct the zig zag along the fearful face of this escarpment. The mountain side falls away dizzily here, and when the engineers made their first preliminary surveys, they had to be lowered down the precipice by ropes to measure their angles. Later, to build the three viaducts that carry the line, the workmen in their turn had to work on the foundations, while dangling suspended by ropes from above."

Over seven hundred men were employed on this section of the line, often referred to as 'the crowning glory' of Whitton's masterpiece. Their lives were not to be envied. Housed in flimsy tent camps that afforded little protection from the elements, and working under dangerous and exposed conditions, the men suffered both the extremes of summer heat and the full force of the icy winds that swept along the edge of the escarpment in winter. Often their only memorial was a journalist's bleak reference to violent death or serious accident.

When the railway was finally opened to traffic on 18 October, 1869, the first train from Sydney descended the western escarpment and arrived in Bowenfels with an absence of public ceremony. "The present timetable", noted the *Sydney Morning*

Whitton's masterpiece, the Great Zig Zag (Blue Mts City Lib.)

Herald, "is simply extended to and from Bowenfels" and only "ordinary" trains were scheduled to run on the opening day.

This quiet reception of Whitton's vision belied the immense impact this achievement was to have on the Blue Mountains in future years. The Great Zig Zag became a popular and internationally recognised attraction. The contrast of its classical elegance with the wild Australian landscape seized the attention of artists and photographers alike.

Ease of travel afforded by the new steam powered railway almost immediately began to broaden the public's perceptions of the value and worth of the Blue Mountains. When the western line was extended to Bathurst in 1876, a new period of settlement and tourism was already underway.

A Royal Rail Excursion

Shortly after the opening of the railway to The Weatherboard, Sydney played host to its first royal visitor when H.R.H. Prince Alfred, Duke of Edinburgh, arrived as Commander of H.M.S. *Galatea* on 22 January, 1868.

On 7 February he was treated, along with "a select party of ladies and gentlemen, present by invitation", to a rail excursion to the Blue Mountains to view The Weatherboard Falls. The Prince's visit did much to popularise the newly accessible Blue Mountains in influential circles of Sydney society.

A month later Prince Alfred's visit to Australia was cut short in dramatic circumstances when he was shot and wounded during a Grand Picnic at Clontarf on Sydney Harbour. The incident unleashed a storm of sectarian bitterness with rumours of Fenian plots and Irish Catholic treachery rife in the community.

The Prince subsequently recovered and left Australia in early April. His would-be assassin, Henry James O'Farrell went to the gallows at Darlinghurst Gaol a week or two later.

In Charles Troedel's 1878 New South Wales Album *the Zig Zag is described in these terms: "The scenery from the line is very grand and the sense of danger which a stranger feels as the train rushes along the edge of the perpendicular declivities, or crosses frowning chasms, imparts a stirring interest to the journey."* Picturesque Atlas of Australasia, *1886. (Blue Mts City Lib.)*

"A luncheon, furnished by Mr Dettman, was served in a large marquee, erected at a distance of about a mile from the station, at 2 o'clock, and after doing justice to the viands and wines the Prince and party visited the Falls. Owing to the late rains there was an unusually large quantity of water tumbling over. It is stated his Royal Highness expressed his admiration of the Falls and surrounding scenery. The party returned to Sydney early in the evening." Illustrated London News, *2 May, 1868. (Blue Mts City Lib.)*

"The engines immediately turned over and rolled down the embankment dragging several trucks with them, throwing everything into inextricable confusion ..." dramatised the Sydney Morning Herald *on the day following the accident on 31 January, 1878. (Mitchell Lib.)*

Midnight Collision

Until duplication of the Mountain line occurred in the early twentieth century, a single line linked the coastal plain with the west. At places along the line crossing points were located where trains waited for the all-clear before proceeding along the next section of track. Wascoe's Siding (now Glenbrook) was the final crossing point for Sydney-bound trains before their descent of the Mountains via the Lapstone Zig Zag.

A little after ten o'clock on the evening of Wednesday, 30 January, 1878, the stationmaster at Penrith received a message from Blue Mountains (now Lawson) that a Special goods train, carrying coal and shale, had just passed and would wait at Wascoe's Siding. Confident of this information, he gave the all-clear to a waiting west-bound goods train

It was from Blue Mountain Railway Station that the fateful message regarding the Special Goods was sent to the stationmaster at Penrith on the evening of Wednesday 30 January, 1878. The station at Blue Mountain opened in 1867 and took its name from the Blue Mountain Inn which had been operating since the 1840s. In 1879 the name of the village and station was changed to Lawson. (Mitchell Lib.)

which now steamed slowly out of Penrith, across the Nepean River and on to Emu Plains.

As the twenty-two wagon train approached the steep climb into the Blue Mountains, its engine's throttle wide open, the driver was astonished to see, some distance ahead, a light moving on the line. Almost as soon as he gave a blast on his whistle both he and his fireman realised with horror that the Sydney-bound goods he expect to 'cross' at Wascoe's Siding had, in fact, gambled on a clear line to Emu Plains and was now hurtling down the final section of Lapstone Hill. "Death", said the *Sydney Morning Herald,* "stared them in the face point blank." Whistles blew and brakes screamed but the impending collision was inevitable.

The railway line over the Blue Mountains has seen some spectacular accidents during its history, but the one that occurred in the final hours of that Wednesday evening was horrific. "The engines immediately turned over", reported the *Herald's* journalist, "and rolled down the embankment dragging several trucks with them, throwing everything into an inextricable confusion ... ." Sparks from the crushed boilers ignited the coal and shale spilled from the wagons of the Sydney-bound train creating "a terribly grand effect in the midnight gloom." The driver and assistant guard of the eastbound train and the fireman of the westbound were killed. The accident, ironically, had occurred immediately opposite the small Emu Plains cemetery.

The Coroner's inquiry and the Government's own Departmental inquiry both revealed the inadequate safe working procedures practiced by the Railways in N.S.W. Three men died before official lethargy was stirred but their deaths lead to the introduction of stricter safety standards.

A Fashionable Refreshment Stop

On early maps Mount Victoria was labelled 'One Tree Hill'. When the railway station was opened as Mount Victoria in 1868 impetus was provided for rapid growth of an important Mountain township.

By the mid-1880s Mount Victoria had become, according to one early guidebook, "a busy thriving country resort" possessing "high-class hotels, stores, boarding-houses, and villa residences". It had also become the fashionable 'refreshment' stop on the journey to Jenolan Caves. Visitors could pause after the long train trip from Sydney, visit Govett's Leap or one of the other local sights, rest the night, then continue their trip to the Caves the following day.

In 1884 this is just what J. Herbert Roberts did:

At about two o'clock we reached Mount Victoria, a very small township, having one large hotel with an imposing tower. In the afternoon I wandered about promiscuously, as I like to do halting now and then to enjoy a particular scene. Around me lay all the signs of tourists' seats, band-stands, and tea-sheds, but, happily, none of the individuals themselves. I got on an insular rock overlooking the Mount Victoria valley — a grand scene, especially bathed, as it was then, in the rich dying glow of the setting sun. All the cows here have tinkling bells hung from their necks, and their music, as they wander about the hills and heard from afar, was very charming, and reminded me of Chamonix. There were a few nice people staying at the hotel, and we spent the evening together in the sitting-room which was homely and comfortable, and warmed by a cheerful fire.

A World Tour. A Year's Diary 1884-85

The following morning, with a companion, he walked out to Govett's Leap, "one of the natural wonders of the Blue Mountains, perhaps of the world". Returning to Mount Victoria for lunch, Roberts continued his rail journey that afternoon, descending the famous Zig Zag and arriving at Tarana, "our starting point to the Fish River Caves", around four o'clock.

Mt Victoria Station was the fashionable refreshment stop of its day and the stepping off point to the Jenolan Caves. By the 1880s it had become a thriving resort with high class hotels and residences. *(ca. 1871, State Rail Authority.)*

It was a sooty ride to the mountains in one of these commodious steam trains, Mt Victoria Station, ca. 1875. (State Rail Authority)

The Passing of the Zig Zags

John Whitton's railway was of light economic construction characterised by steep grades and tight curves. As time went by and use increased, considerable relocation occurred to ease grades and straighten curves. Numerous abandoned cuttings and formations remain today as evidence of this refinement.

Visible modifications occurred on the eastern and western escarpments where the magnificent zig zags were replaced with a more efficient system of tunnels. As traffic on the western line became heavier and the volume of freight increased, both zig zags began to experience serious bottlenecks. These were aggravated by the shortness of the reversing stations which imposed an unacceptable limit on the length of trains.

The first change of any note occurred at Lapstone at the end of 1892. A new line was opened which bypassed the zig zag and incorporated a tunnel through Lapstone Hill. The construction of this tunnel was painted by Arthur Streeton in his famous *Fire's On.* This tunnel was not a success, being tight and badly ventilated and causing great discomfort to both crew and passengers. An alternative was necessary.

By the turn of the century, serious thought was being given to phasing out the Great Zig Zag. No amount of minor modification was able to prevent the gradual strangulation of train movement at this point on the western line. In 1908, work started on an ambitious alternative to 'Whitton's Masterpiece' which required the construction of a system of ten tunnels, close together and linked by deep cuttings.

The new route, described by one writer as a series of "ratholes" deep within the mountain, was eventually opened to traffic in October 1910. Immediately the western line saw an improvement

in efficiency. The running time was cut by almost twenty-five minutes between Sydney and Bowenfels and timetables had to be quickly adjusted.

At the end of 1910 the plant employed on the 'ten tunnel' deviation was moved to Glenbrook where work on the replacement of the earlier deviation now became the priority. Then Glenbrook Gorge deviation was a major undertaking involving cutting a shelf for the double track out of the huge wall of rock that rose, almost perpendicularly from the bottom of the gorge. It also required a tunnel through The Bluff and the abandonment of the original Knapsack Viaduct for a new curved, brick one lower down the gully.

The deviation work on both flanks of the Blue Mountains required the employment of large numbers of navvies, creating a temporary population explosion in Mount Victoria and Glenbrook. The navvies, took their name from their British antecedents who had worked as 'navigators' on the construction of canals. These men laboured on the foundation work and laid the tracks. By 1910 the workforce in the west had grown to around 1500. In 1912 there were some 800 men on the books at Glenbrook.

Apart from the dangerous nature of his work, the life of a navvy and his family was unsettled. They lived an itinerant existence, chasing the work from place to place, staying in large temporary camps. Iron roofed shacks with whitewashed hessian walls sprang

Workers pose for a photograph during the construction of the currently operating Glenbrook Tunnel, ca. 1910. (Blue Mts City Lib.)

Railway workers camp in what is now Emu Road, Glenbrook. Construction of Glenbrook Gorge Deviation, ca. 1911. (Nolan Family/Blue Mts City Lib.)

up in proximity to the work site and disappeared as quickly when the job was finished.

Between 1911 and 1913 there were three camps at the Glenbrook site, the largest spread along what is now Emu Road at The Bluff. This was Main Camp and it boasted its own hotel and community hall. The 'Union Hall' was the scene of numerous dances and musical evenings while the pub supplied the local constabulary with a regular supply of 'drunk and disorderlies'.

The deviation at Glenbrook was completed in 1913, the new 'down' line opening in May. By September the route around the Gorge was in full operation and the old line closed down. Over a decade later, the Great Western Highway was re-routed up the eastern escarpment using the path of the old railway to Blaxland.

Frederick Eccleston Du Faur (1832-1915) whose vision encompassed the opening up of this spectacular region "to tourist and artists" and the encouragement of its use as "a healthy field of exercise for the young men of our own city." (Blue Mts Hist. Soc.)

"Du Faur's Blue Mountains craze"

Frederick Eccleston Du Faur, Chief Draftsman in the Crown Lands Office in the 1870s and a noted patron of the arts and sciences, formed a strong attachment to the Blue Mountains landscape "which,

for sublimity or grandeur, is not to be surpassed in the world." His vision encompassed the opening up of this spectacular region "to tourists and artists" and the encouragement of its use as "a healthy field of exercise for the young men of our own city." His enthusiasm, fuelled by numerous visits, was expressed widely and discussion of "Du Faur's Blue Mountains craze" was heard regularly in the salons of Sydney society.

While others, like Parkes and his friends, were attracted to more accessible regions closer to the new railway line, Du Faur purchased land in 1875 at remote and beautiful Mount Wilson. He had no plans for a country home. To facilitate the pursuit of his cultural and scientific interests (he was a member of the Royal Society of N.S.W., a founder of the Geographical Society of Australia and an original member of the N.S.W. Academy of Art) he employed a caretaker to maintain a rough mountain hut there,

Du Faur purchased land at Mt Wilson in 1875 where his caretaker, Lewis Thompson, maintained this rough mountain hut. (Blue Mts Hist. Soc.)

Bischoff, in dark clothes and cap, and Piguenit, in white shirt, in the Grose Valley in 1875 (Blue Mts Hist. Soc.)

replete with equipment and pack-horses. His caretaker was Lewis Thompson, sole survivor of an earlier, ill-fated expedition, organised by Du Faur and led by Andrew Hume, that had sought to unravel the mystery of Ludwig Leichhardt's disappearance.

From the Mount Wilson hut Du Faur mounted his regular excursions into the Grose Valley and surrounding ranges. In 1875 he established a camp in the Grose Valley about fifteen kilometres from the Hartley Vale siding. This was reached via a track originally constructed by surveyors assessing the region for construction of a railway in 1857. Du Faur re-opened the track which had become obstructed by fallen trees, landslips and undergrowth.

A second camp was established about eight

Members of the Du Faur Expedition including Du Faur and his camp keepers in 1875. (Blue Mts Hist. Soc.)

kilometres further down the Grose at its confluence with Govetts Leap Creek, below Mount King George. For this second camp, to enable artistic and photographic equipment to be transported to within sight of Govett's Leap, a track was blazed to 'Smoke Rock' from which "an excellent view of all three cascades is obtained". A number of trees disrupting the view were removed from the vicinity of each camp.

Through his encouragement, artists and photographers like William Piguenit and Joseph Bischoff visited the Grose Valley in 1875. The camps had been established for this and Du Faur hoped that their work would influence others to enjoy healthy adventure offered by the "wildest grandest and most beautiful scenery in New South Wales".

In a letter to the *Sydney Morning Herald*, written while Piguenit and Bischoff were still in the valley, he said: "It may be mentioned that at the time of my leaving the camp on Monday last, Mr Piguenit, who had then spent three weeks in the valley, had secured about 15 subjects. Sketching them in water colours, he intends reproducing them in oils; and he will have had the first opportunity of illustrating our mountain scenery from the points where it can be studied to the best advantage, i.e., from the bottom of its gorges, instead of the summit of its ranges ... Mr Piguenit and Mr Bischoff, the landscape photographer, will probably remain in the valley for another ten days, and quit it with regret ... ." (October 1875)

Following the departure of Piguenit and Bischoff, Du Faur arranged for Lewis Thompson to remain in the valley for several weeks to afford an opportunity for "any gentlemen interested in mountain scenery (either as an artist or mere spectator) who may care to carry his swag of blankets down to the camp. A plentiful supply of provisions will be provided, and each visitor can settle with the campkeeper in charge for the accommodation afforded him, canvas and bark shelter will be provided for about thirty people."

Included among those who took up this invitation were the artists James Howe Carse and Henry Grant Lloyd.

In 1874 Du Faur was chosen as one of the official observers on the Blue Mountains to observe the Transit of Venus expected on December 9 and last observed in 1769 by Captain James Cook. Of the four Government Astronomical Stations established, this one at Woodford was set up in the seven hectare former police paddock to the west of Alfred Fairfax's Woodford House. Observation of the passage of the planet Venus between the sun and the earth was successfully accomplished. (Blue Mts City Lib.)

Mount Wilson — A fashionable mountain retreat

In the 1870s, at the same time as the Faulconbridge-Springwood area was attracting the attention of Sir Henry Parkes and his friends, the more remote location of Mount Wilson was also gaining a reputation as a fashionable mountain retreat.

On the recommendation of Frederick Eccleston Du Faur, the area, named after the then Minister for Lands John Bowie Wilson, was surveyed in 1868 and in 1870 sixty-two portions of land were offered for sale. By the mid-1880s a close-knit community of families had formed and the names of Merewether, Cox, Gregson, Hay, Wynne and Stephen all became identified with 'The Mount'. A post office, general store and cricket ground were built before the end of the decade and in 1891 a public school was opened.

During the hot summer months these families sought refuge in their tranquil country hideaways glorified with names like 'Dennarque', 'Campanella', 'Nooroo', 'Bebeah', 'Yengo' and 'Beowang'. Their spiritual home was England and the cool mountain climate and rich basaltic soil provided an ideal environment in which to cultivate the English style gardens they admired. Oaks and elms, lilacs and rhododendrons, daffodils and bluebells were all planted in the early years.

The keen desire for seclusion and coolness meant none of the early homes in Mount Wilson were positioned with the surrounding views in mind. Their gardens were designed to enhance the sense of sanctuary by enclosing the houses completely. The wider mountain landscape was something to be experienced outside the household environs from community lookouts such as Wynne's or Du Faur's Rocks.

The 'lost world' character of Mount Wilson — a mixture of the tropics and "dear old England" —

The celebrated Wynne Prize for landscape painting has an appropriate association with Mount Wilson. Richard Wynne built a small cottage here in 1875 followed by the extensive 'Yarrawa' recorded in the 1880s as thriving with fruit and flowers. It has remained in the family for over 100 years. (Blue Mts Hist. Soc.)

was noted by many visitors. One, writing in the *Blue Mountains Echo* in 1913, described the experience of coming upon this "veritable Garden of Eden" hidden in the midst of "rugged Mountain country". It was now the age of the motor car but things had changed little since the early years.

Mount Wilson is still remote, off the beaten path and it continues to offer the serenity early residents looked forward to every time they left the train at the Mount Wilson platform (now Bell) and boarded their sulkies for the long ride into the village.

St George's Anglican Church, Mount Wilson

The Anglican Church of St George stands among its congregation of tree ferns at the corner of The Avenue and Church Lane in Mount Wilson. Built on land donated by the Wynne family, the church was consecrated in 1913 as a memorial to the successful Sydney merchant Marcus Clark who had come to live on the Mount in 1910. The Church of St George was the fulfilment of a wish Clark had expressed in the last years of his life. Prior to its erection, religious services had been held in one or other of the private residences and later in the public school. Today, the church is included among the parish responsibilities of the rector at St Aidan's in Blackheath and, once a month, the sounds of the Anglican liturgy blend harmoniously with the old world memories that survive in this isolated part of the Blue Mountains.

St George's Anglican Church. (Blue Mts City Lib.)

"*Strange winged insects dashed their gauzy wings against the glass window of the car, demanding admittance; a flock of gaily-plumaged parrots flew screaming overhead, and a silver pheasant, startled by the rush of the car, flew past and sought refuge in the dark lonely scrub that clothed the Mountain side. It seemed like dreamland—and that instead of being on one of the highest peaks of the Blue Mountains, one had been suddenly transported to the far off islands of the South Seas.*" Blue Mountains Echo, *1913. Photographer Harry Phillips. (Blue Mts City Lib.)*

Sir Henry's Country Residence

In the 1870s and 1880s the wealthy and prominent citizen's country residences began to transform the landscape of regions as far apart as Springwood and Mount Wilson. Businessmen, politicians, lawyers and academics rushed to participate in what became known as 'the Blue Mountains Craze'.

In the Springwood region the foremost of these affluent refugees from the city was Sir Henry Parkes. The young Parkes emigrated to Australia with his wife Clarinda in 1839. In Sydney, he worked as a labourer, as a dealer in 'fancy' goods and as a newspaper proprietor. By the mid-1850s he was well on his way to becoming a leading light on the colonial scene. He was to become Premier of N.S.W. five times and, as a principal advocate of Federation, exerted enormous influence upon the course of Australia's history. He was knighted in 1877.

In the mid-1870s Parkes purchased land in the Blue Mountains and constructed a country retreat which he named Faulconbridge House in honour of his mother, Martha Faulconbridge.

His example was followed and from the mid-1870s to the early 1880s most of the land between Faulconbridge and Linden was owned by Sir Henry and a coterie of his influential friends. These included Sir James Martin, Sir Alfred Stephen, and Professor Charles Badham who all set about enthusiastically building their mountain homes, cultivating gardens and orchards, and laying out walking tracks to nearby lookouts and the surrounding gullies.

When Sir Henry and Lady Parkes played host to the young Prince Albert and Prince George (later King George V) during their visit to Australia in 1881 the *Sydney Morning Herald* on 21 July, 1881 described the Parkes estate at Faulconbridge in the following terms:

> The grounds at Faulconbridge present a series of steep terraces, trying enough to the youngest limbs, yet after breakfast Sir Henry Parkes led the way over them with an agility which sorely tried the powers of the Princes and other members of the party who followed his leadership. A pretty tree-fern gully spanned by rustic bridges was perhaps for the visitors, the most attractive scene Faulconbridge could show; and the multitude of rare flowers, delicate ferns, and curious orchids which sprang from the crevices of the rocks and tree stumps around, elicited expressions of the liveliest admiration from people who had been accustomed in England to see only the hardier varieties of these plants, and then when they were tended in hot-houses. (21 July 1881)

A later visitor remarked that the extensive gardens and landscaping told "of a man with large ideas ... of a man with a soul above huckstering." ('The Globe Trotter', *Australian Gossip and Story*.)

By 1887 Parkes' money problems had led to the

Sir Henry Parkes strolls around his country residence at Faulconbridge with his dog Maori, n.d. (Springwood Hist. Soc.)

assigning of his Faulconbridge estate and the dividing up of his mountain property. His friends fared little better. By 1882 Sir Alfred Stephen was finding the expense of maintaining a country home too great and sold up; Sir James Martin's dreams for his Numantia estate ended in the auction rooms in 1884; and Professor Badham's death that same year led to the sale of his property.

When Parkes died in 1896 his family declined the pomp and ceremony of a State funeral. The event still attracted a vast array of dignitaries and citizens and the mourners filled six carriages of the special funeral train that bore his body from the Sydney Mortuary Station to Faulconbridge. There he was laid to rest beside his wife Clarinda in the small cemetery he had earlier set aside from his estate as sacred ground.

The funeral cortege of Sir Henry Parkes arriving at Central Station, Sydney on 29 April 1896. (Springwood Hist. Soc.)

Lilianfels — "A high-class cottage"

In the 1880s a number of wealthy and influential people acquired land in the Blue Mountains and built substantial houses for their families. Among them was Dublin-born Sir Frederick Matthew Darley, Chief Justice and Lieutenant-Governor of NSW, 'one of the noblest figures to sit on the Australian bench'.

In 1888 Darley purchased twelve acres close to Echo Point, Katoomba, within view of the magnificent Jamison Valley. He engaged Varney Parkes, the architect son of his friend Sir Henry Parkes, to design and build a 'high-class cottage' as a summer residence which he later named 'Lilianfels' in honour of his daughter Lilian Darley. 'Fels' is the German word meaning 'high rocky ground'. It is the

The sweeping gravel driveway was a main feature of 'Lilianfels' giving a feeling of space and grandeur to the house. On the edge of the formal garden can be seen a grassed slope with a fence below, this unique aspect of garden landscaping is termed a Ha-Ha. The Ha-Ha allowed garden designers to dispense with walls for keeping cattle, horses or deer from the garden, and encouraged them to consider the whole landscape as part of the garden design. This photo was taken by Harry Phillips. (Blue Mts Hist. Soc.)

only house designed by Varney Parkes surviving in the upper Blue Mountains.

Lilian Darley, described as 'the beauty of the family' was popular in Sydney's social circles. The family had already rented premises in the district hoping the fresh mountain air would cure Lilian of tuberculosis. Sadly she died in April 1889, aged 22, before the residence which bore her name was completed early in the following year.

Darley spared no expense on the house and landscaping. He took a keen interest in horticulture and planted evergreen trees and shrubs in profusion for verdure and shade. Clipped hedges and a

sweeping circular drive edged with exotic annuals and perennials were the main feature of the landscaping. He also created a flourishing orchard, watered by a windmill pump which fed water from an underground spring, and a formal sunken garden.

Built of timber with a slate roof in the style of the period 'Lilianfels' has several eccentric features such as the split-level upstairs rooms with dormer windows incorporated in the multi-angled roof. The interior walls are mainly lath-and-plaster, with imitation cedar panelling in the downstairs reception room. The rooms have panelled ceilings of Baltic pine. Other unusual features are the stained-glass

windows whose main motif is a cuckoo, glazed terra-
cotta chimney pots and brass lightning conductors.

In the following years Darley acquired more land
and extended the grounds to twenty-two acres. A
coachhouse and stables, a tennis court and a
caretaker's lodge were added.

The family used the house between 1890 and 1908
entertaining many distinguished visitors among them
Queen Mary when she was Duchess of York in
Federation year 1901.

*Sir Frederick Matthew Darley, G.C.M.C., 6th Chief
Justice of N.S.W., 1886-1910, was the original owner
of 'Lilianfels' in Katoomba. He served five terms as
Lieutenant-Governor of N.S.W. and is here pictured
in the costume in which he swore in Australia's first
Governor-General, Lord Hopetoun, on the 5 January,
1901. (Mitchell Lib.)*

*This photo showing a garden fete at Lilianfels ca. 1914 is a Harry Phillips photo. During the Kemp
ownership 1912-1920 many such fetes were held for various charity fund raising efforts: Red Cross War
effort, Katoomba Presbyterian Church, Y.M.C.A. and Wounded Soldier's Fund. (Blue Mts Hist. Soc.)*

In 1908 'Lilianfels' was sold to George Begg
Vickery a Sydney merchant and owner of the Mt
Keira coal mine near Wollongong. Sir Frederick and
his wife returned to Ireland where he enjoyed a brief
retirement before he died in London in 1910 in his
eightieth year.

Like their predecessors, the Vickerys maintained
'Lilianfels' strictly as a summer residence before
selling it five years later to Alexander Albert Kemp,
founder of the Drug Company of Australia. The
Kemp family were the first owners to use 'Lilianfels'
as a permanent residence, opening the house and
grounds to the public on many occasions to raise
money for the war effort. The Prince of Wales called

The Katoomba Waltz

The rediscovery, in 1989, of Mary McCarron Maguire's *Katoomba Waltz* has led to speculation about a 'lost school' of popular composers whose works were inspired by the natural splendours of the Blue Mountains. Published in 1895, *The Katoomba Waltz* is dedicated to Sir Frederick Darley (then Lieutenant Governor of New South Wales) and Lady Darley who lived in 'Lilianfels'.

The Katoomba Waltz was first performed at Government House in Sydney. The *Sydney Morning Herald* pronounced it 'a dashing composition admirably suited to ballroom purposes.' Soon after this, the waltz appeared on variety programmes at

'Lilianfels' during the Kemp ownership. (Blue Mts City Lib.)

*The cover of the sheet music to Katoomba Waltz.
(Blue Mts City Lib.)*

at the house when he visited the Blue Mountains in 1920.

In 1921 the house was sold to the Joynton-Smith Trust Fund, Sir James Joynton-Smith, MLC, publisher of *Smith's Weekly,* being the principal partner. Two years later the estate was subdivided into thirty-four blocks leaving the house on two acres. From 1923 to 1952 'Lilianfels' was owned by Samuel G. Baker, a Sydney manufacturer, who leased the house to several different people who operated it as a guest house. The place was well patronised and many people revisiting the house in recent years recall fond memories of holidays at 'Lilianfels'.

In 1952 Wladislaw Ujma, a Polish water-construction engineer bought the house and continued to lease it for use as a guest house. After

his death twelve years later his wife Zofia occupied 'Lilianfels' where she lived as a semi-recluse until 1986. During this period the house and grounds fell into disrepair although in 1984, when 'Lilianfels' was classified by the Heritage Council, some stabilising repairs were carried out.

In 1987 'Lilianfels' was purchased by Derani Pty Ltd who planned to restore the house and build an eighty-five room guest house on adjacent land but were unable to attract investors and were forced to sell. In August 1990, a tree-planting ceremony marked the beginning of restoration and construction work by the new owners, Nara Pty Ltd, a Japanese company.

Colin Slade

Sydney's famous Tivoli Theatre was added to the repertoire of the N.S.W. Artillery's Regimental Band.

Little is known about the waltz's composer. Mary McCarron Maguire published two other waltzes, *The Antonina* and *The Commonwealth* during the decade 1890-1900. *The Commonwealth Waltz*, evidently inspired by the coming of Federation in 1901, earned Mary a lampoon in the form of a mock-heroic poem in *The Bulletin*. A few lines give the flavour of the poem:

'Mary McCarron Maguire!
... my soul leaps to flame at the sound of her name,
And there's no knowing what may transpire.'

Mary was a gently-reared young woman of Edgecliff, and her family were frequent guests at Admiralty House. The suggestiveness of *The Bulletin's* poem was probably offensive to the family and to Mary. It remains a mystery why *The Bulletin* chose to satirise the composer in this way. Mary didn't publish any more music, and her life is hard to trace from the sparse mementoes held by the National Library.

Two other musical items dating from the approximate period 1890-1910 are a mazurka, *Leura Falls*, by Alicia Nolan, and *The Cascade Waltz*, by Louis L. Howarde. Undoubtedly there are others, reflecting a period when Australians were beginning to come of age culturally, and pay tribute to their uniquely beautiful environment.

Kerry Leves

The Carrington

It is not generally known that the development of Katoomba as a tourist and residential centre was mainly due to The Carrington being located there instead of at Wentworth Falls as originally intended. During the 1870s the Hon. James Henry Neale M.L.A. acquired a large tract of land which is now the site of the main business centre of Katoomba. After subdivision of the grant in 1879, by the syndicate who

The Carrington during Goyder's ownership.
(Blue Mts City Lib.)

The Carrington Hotel,

KATOOMBA, BLUE MOUNTAINS.

Situate 66 miles from Sydney, at an elevation of 3333 feet. Admitted to be the Best Hotel on the Mountains.

TARIFF - 10s. & 11s. per Day.   £2 2s. to £3 3s. per Week.

Katoomba is now connected with Sydney by Telephone, and any Exchange in Sydney can be rung up from the Carrington Office. Cost: 1s. 6d. for 3 minutes, and 1s. for each additional 3 minutes.

had earlier been refused an offer to buy prime land at Wentworth Falls, the hotel site was bought by Mr Harry Rowell, a Sydney hotelier.

Plans were drawn by architect C. Kirkpatrick, and F. Drewett of Lithgow won the contract for the construction of sixty rooms — the original section of the grand building, which dwarfed the little mining settlement. The hotel, then known as The Great Western, was opened in 1882 and has continued to dominate Katoomba for over a century. In 1886 the property was sold by Mr Rowell's widow to Mr F. C. Goyder, a squatter from Queensland and the first

A chimney-less Carrington Hotel and paddocks on the corner of Katoomba and Main Streets seen from Hudson's Gully, now Kingsford Smith Park, about 1890. Photo by G. Kitch (Mitchell Lib.)

Katoomba in the 1880s with The Carrington dominating the hill in the background, the railway turntable in the foreground and the gatehouse on the right at the level crossing. (Blue Mts City Lib.)

mayor of Katoomba, who immediately set about adding wings to the hotel, doubling its accommodation. He improved the facilities and standard of the hotel, and changed its name to The Carrington in honour of the then Governor of N.S.W., Lord Carrington, a frequent guest.

The popularity and prestige of The Carrington continued to increase, and before the turn of the century Mr Goyder employed Mr A. L. Peacock to assist in the management. By 1902 Peacock had leased The Carrington from Goyder, and remained as host for the ensuing decade. In 1905 he advertised the establishment as "The largest and best known Tourist Hotel in the Southern Hemisphere". Mr Peacock was civic minded and (like his predecessor F. C. Goyder) served as an alderman on the Katoomba Municipal Council. He was instrumental in achieving the installation of water and sewerage systems in the town — as well as providing "a splendid service of lavatories, baths and water closets upon each floor" of his magnificent hotel!

During the period of Peacock's lease wealthy newspaper magnate, James Joynton Smith, became interested in The Carrington and began lengthy negotiations to purchase the property. He already owned The Imperial at Mount Victoria, and was later

On Monday 9 June, 1930, Amy Johnson, who had just become the first woman to fly solo from England to Australia, arrived at the Carrington at 1 p.m. Hundreds of people gathered greeted 'Johnny' as she came out of the Carrington and an open touring car was obtained to carry her on a triumphant tour around the town. The Blue Mountains Star 14 June, 1930 reported that: "Standing up on the front seat with her back to the windscreen she greeted the people with that winning smile of hers and continually waved her hand." (Blue Mts Hist. Soc. both photos)

approached by Mark Foy to take a lease of the Hydro Majestic at Medlow Bath, thus gaining control of the three largest hotels on the mountains. By 1913 Joynton Smith had established a powerhouse at the rear of The Carrington, necessitating the erection of the now famous tapering octagonal chimney stack, to provide electricity for the hotel, and also the town of Katoomba. That service, later extended to other mountain towns, was maintained until 1925 when a powerhouse was erected in Bent Street by local government authorities.

Joynton Smith added further rooms to The Carrington, and altered the original appearance with an Art Nouveau facade. The former verandah was enclosed with an undulating Italianate balcony surmounting a wall of beautifully designed stained glass which prompted the original classification of the building by the National Trust on 3 July 1978. The last major alteration to The Carrington was in

1927 when a further wing was added to bring the number of bedrooms to 200. Many famous guests, including members of the Royal family, have enjoyed the grand atmosphere of The Carrington over the years. The huge columned dining room, also rich in stained glass, is very impressive with its fine chandeliers and furnishings.

Following the Second World War, and the subsequent decline in tourism on the Blue Mountains, The Carrington gradually lost its patronage and fell into disrepair. In 1985 it was closed by order of the Licensing Court, and has since been the subject of a Government enquiry regarding its re-opening.

With its spacious grounds and commanding position high above the town this faded edifice remains the largest man-made feature on the Blue Mountains.

Gwen Silvey

An official party outside The Carrington in 1907 on the occasion of the opening of Katoomba's first water supply. The Governor, Sir Harry Rowson, is in the front seat. Speaking to him is the manager of The Carrington, A.L.Peacock. Katoomba's Mayor, Alderman H.Goyder, is in the back seat with the Governor's Aide-De-Campe. (Blue Mts City Lib. both photos)

Mark Foy combined the elegant Belgravia Hotel and the residence of Edward Hargreaves who discovered gold in Australia, with another smaller cottage and a domed casino imported from Chicago to form his extensive long establishment. (Blue Mts Hist. Soc.)

Hydro Majestic

The Hydro Majestic was opened on 4th July, 1904 in the middle of a snow storm — four days before Sydney was first lit by electricity — The Hydropathic Establishment overlooking Megalong Valley at Medlow Bath was way ahead of its time. It had privately operated electricity, sewerage and telephone systems for its own use, as well as walking tracks and various sporting facilities for guests. As one early visitor commented "The conception of the place was daring and brilliant enough for Monte Cristo himself."

Mark Foy had combined the elegant Belgravia Hotel and the residence of Edward Hargreaves (the discoverer of gold in Australia), together with another smaller cottage, and a dome-roofed casino building imported from Chicago, to form a complex 300 metres long.

Most of the food requirements were produced on farms down in Megalong Valley — the produce being brought up the cliff face by flying fox, and stored in the Hydro's own freezing works.

On opening day Foy ran the first guests up the mountain by car — a great novelty — as was the revolving searchlight which was mounted on the building. It was powered by the electricity supply installed at the Hydro to service the village of Medlow as well as the establishment. The dining room waiters were Chinese, and coffee was served by two small Turks in national costume.

Resident Dr. Bauer from Switzerland saw patients who abided by a strict set of rules which included no alcohol, no tobacco, and no discussion of maladies. The many watery techniques available at the Hydro in those early days involved electrotherapy, abdomen packs, back sponging and back spouting. Some of these in water as hot as could be borne. From Baden Baden in Europe, Mark Foy imported spa water which was stored in copper tanks, giving it a most unpleasant flavour. It was consumed in large quantities by the guests for the sake of their health.

After several years the bath treatments, having failed in popularity, were discontinued, but the drinking of the spa water was still endured by many world famous celebrities who attended the Hydro.

Famous people who visited the Hydro include German heiress Bertha Krupp, and Tommy Burns for whom a cottage was specially built in 1908 to house his trainer and masseurs. Prime Minister Edmund Barton died during a visit in 1920. Nellie Melba and Clara Butt sang in the Casino.

In 1922 a disastrous fire swept through the Hydro, and burnt away 100 metres of the building, including the Belgravia Hotel section. A total of 130 bedrooms were lost in the fire.

A new wing, to replace the old Belgravia which had been burned, was built in 1938. During the Second World War the Hydro was used as a convalescent hospital for the walking wounded of the United States Army in which time the hotel suffered its own war wound when the hotel's goat herd, statues in the grounds and light fittings were all pot-shotted in wild west fashion.

Recently altered and refurbished, the Hydro Majestic, with its wonderful views over the Megalong Valley, still maintains its place as one of the best known resort hotels on the Blue Mountains.

Gwen Silvey

The elegant Belgravia Hotel which was burned down in the fire of 1922. (Blue Mts City Lib.)

1913 celebrations of the Centenary of the Crossing of the Blue Mountains. (Mitchell Lib.)

This photo taken at 'Sheleagh Cottage', Medlow Bath, ca. 1938, shows 'Amah' Wong Ah Tong standing beside the young girl Mary Shaw granddaughter of Mark Foy. Wong Ah Tong was brought out from Malaya by Mary's father as a nanny to his children (Mary Shaw)

This photo ca. 1904 shows a Chinese waiter with guests in the long gallery at the Hydro Majestic Hotel at Medlow Bath. An early newspaper reported that when the Hydro was opened, "Chinese waiters waited on each table and two little Turks dressed in their national costume poured coffee in the lounge." (Jim Smith)

Guests outside the Hydro Majestic preparing to depart for a drive around the mountain sights.
(Jim Smith/Blue Mts City Lib.)

RIGHT: *The sign on the cart reads, "Jimmy War Sing, Market Gardener and Fruiterer, Katoomba." (ca. 1902). Jimmy ran a market garden for several years in the first decade of this century at Katoomba. The garden was situated in a natural gully with a small watercourse running through it behind Loftus and Neale Streets. It was known as McRae's Paddock and is now waste land owned by the City Council. Several other Chinese market gardeners worked this land also, up until the early 1930s. Older residents remember Jimmy as a kind man who loved children, apparently married but having no children of his own. He would give presents of filled ginger jars to his customers at Christmas. The caption on this photo, "Nicee wegable missee" sadly reflects the unsympathetic attitude and prejudice shown by many towards the Chinese at the time. (Mitchell Lib.)*

LEFT: *'Charlie' or Louie Goh Mong who worked for Mark Foy for thirty-five years at the Hydro Majestic and his Bellevue Hill home. Foy wrote on the back of the photograph: "The most wonderful man I ever knew of any sort — I got him off a vegetable cart. He could cook. He could play billiards and beat you if you wanted him to do it — take and develop and print photos. Knew the bottles when labels were washed off — anyhow he couldn't read labels — was known everywhere and idolised by guests at the Hydro — knew how many pieces of sugar guests took in their coffee even if they returned after absence of two years — always happy and laughing. Took over cleaning of the whole of the galleries — he won a heap of money on Chinese ticket in lottery and went to China, got married — and came back to some northern port and walked over to Sydney and turned up and delighted everyone. Dear old Charlie — nature and God is sure to reward Charlie." (Mary Shaw)*

This photo was taken in 1943 at 12 Hope Street, Katoomba, showing Mr Mar, his wife Mrs So-Hin Mar and in order of age, Albert Vincent, William (standing behind their father) May Valda, Gordon Stanley John, and the baby Keith Peter. Albert Vincent and William Mar attended Katoomba High School. Mr Leong Wah Mar was the Managing Director of the Wing Sang export company of Sydney and served for several years as the President of the Chinese-Australian Society of Sydney. Mr Mar, along with several other Chinese, moved their families to Katoomba because of the impending threat of a Japanese invasion of Sydney during World War II, returning after the war to carry on their businesses. (Dr Mar).

Chinese People in the Blue Mountains

As the western goldfields declined many Chinese, unable to return home drifted into the larger country towns and reverted to their old trades as storekeepers, cooks, servants and market gardeners. By introducing the agricultural style of their homeland — small holdings growing vegetables and fruit — the Chinese contributed to these communities much of whose fresh vegetables had to be brought in (or home grown) until the Chinese came.

This was the pattern in the Blue Mountains. Market gardens were established in Mt Victoria, Megalong Valley, Blackheath, Katoomba and Hazelbrook, and probably in other mountain towns. The largest recorded market garden was at Blackheath on the site of the present-day golf links where as many as twelve Chinese worked the land and grew enough cabbages and cauliflowers not only for the local market but for the Sydney markets also.

Several fruit and vegetable shops run by Chinese existed at Blackheath, and Chinese waiters and cooks were employed at the famous Hydro Majestic Hotel. The last recorded market garden, existing until the early 1930s, was at Katoomba in a stream-fed gully known as MacCrae's Paddock, near the present-day Katoomba Falls caravan park.

The census of 1891, local rate books and newspaper articles provide many interesting stories and names of Chinese who lived in the Blue Mountains. One of these was the Chinese nanny, Amah, Wong Ah Tong, employed to take care of a granddaughter of Mark Foy, owner of the Hydro Majestic.

Although Chinese people lived and worked in the Blue Mountains for about fifty years, next to nothing of material structures or objects survive as reminders. Several discoveries of Chinese ginger jars, whiskey and wine bottles, and an original woven bamboo coolie hat seem to be the sum total of artefacts that have come to light in other country towns.

Luckily, there are enough documents, newspaper articles, oral history recordings by older residents (along with some photos) to give a fair insight into the presence of the early Chinese people in the Blue Mountains, enabling us to investigate their previously unrecognised, or glossed-over contribution to the history of the Blue Mountains.

Colin Slade

"The old charioteer and poet" Mrs Edith Rowsell took this photograph of Peckman with a 2A Brownie Box camera in 1927 outside Balmoral House in Katoomba. Her son Trevor is in the carriage. (Mrs Marion Brodrick, Blue Mts City Lib.)

*An ad for Peckman Brothers, 1887.
(Blue Mts City Lib.)*

Harry Peckman — Blue Mountains Poet

Henry ("Harry") Peckman, "The Blue Mountains Poet", was born at Kurrajong Heights in 1846 and spent his long life in the Blue Mountains. At the age of fourteen he went to Hartley to work as a 'junior useful' for a local hotel keeper. During the pre-railway days of the 1860s, he drove wagons and coaches over the rough mountain road between Penrith and Hartley, sometimes acting as an emergency driver for Cobb & Co. In the 1870s, after the railway had crossed the Mountains, he also began driving visitors to various local 'sights'.

In the 1880s he and his brother John established livery stables in Katoomba. In 1889, he began the first daily coach service from Katoomba to Jenolan Caves. In the late nineteenth century and early twentieth century Peckman's skills as a guide and knowledge of the region were sought after by visitors both titled and common. An excursion with Harry meant performances en route from his extensive repertoire of songs and recitations. Covering subjects as various as the nineteenth century rowing hero Edward Trickett, the Boer War and his beloved Blue Mountains.

After World War I he experienced hard times and watched as the age of the combustion engine gradually rendered his coach and pair obsolete. He died in 1934 and is buried in Katoomba cemetery.

This is the first stanza of his *Katoomba Awake* published in the *Katoomba Times* on 9 November 1884.

Katoomba awake! for the morning is breaking.
Which breathes the glad tidings the future is bright;
Dark night, on her damp wings, her swift flight has taken.
While Goddess Aurora comes forth with the light.
Now dances bright Sol o'er the blue-mantled mountains.
O'erleaping bold ramparts and crags near and far;
The sweet lyre-bird sings with a thousand wild fountains.
While Nature unfolds the superb waratah.
The new virgin Summer is softly subduing.
Old Winter's fierce heroes — then up and be doing!

Katoomba — "Queen City of the Hills"

In its early years Katoomba laid no claim to the status it later achieved among the Mountain towns. While there had been an inn at Pulpit Hill from the 1830s, the town's real beginnings were with the railway. During the 1870s the area was known as The Crushers, the name of the quarry established there to supply the railway with ballast. Trains from the west also found The Crushers a convenient location to adjust their loads before embarking on the steep descent to Penrith.

Towards the end of the 1870s, this lonely mountain outpost began to change dramatically. An official name change to Katoomba occurred in 1878, the same year that businessman, John Britty North, registered his coal mine at the base of the cliffs near Orphan Rock. Within a year the high quality of his coal was winning recognition at the Sydney International Exhibition and the small settlement of Katoomba was considered an important mining centre.

While North was developing his mining enterprise the leaders of Sydney society also began casting their eyes in the direction of Katoomba. The 1870s had seen the popularity of areas like Springwood-Faulconbridge and Mount Wilson as locations for country retreats. The 1880s and 1890s were the beginnings of an era of hotels and guesthouses, centred principally in the upper Mountains at Katoomba.

In 1882 the building of The Great Western Hotel marked the emergence of Katoomba as more than a mining town. Re-christened The Carrington four years later, after patronage by the then Governor-General, the hotel reflected the upgrading of the town.

Throughout the 1880s shops, schools, churches and a local newspaper appeared and in 1889 the town was gazetted as a municipality. Its first Council was elected in January 1890. It governed a socially

Katoomba Street, untarred, looking north, by G. Kitch, ca. 1890s, showing the Methodist Church on the right, which was opened on 9 November, 1888. The first Minister was the Rev. W. Orton. The church is now part of the Uniting Church in Australia. (Blue Mts Hist. Soc.)

annexed town — at one extreme a working class mining centre, at the other, a fashionable and well-to-do resort.

The early tourists who arrived during the 1880s and 1890s were primarily from the privileged classes. They stayed in gracious comfort at stylish establishments like The Carrington, The Leura Coffee Palace (later The Ritz) or The Balmoral and sought the mysteries of Nature along winding bush tracks. They had money and leisure time and the Blue Mountains offered a 'hill station' retreat from the

pressures of the political and business world of Sydney.

By the turn of the century economic and social changes were occurring in the wider Australian community which began to produce a more affluent and mobile middle class. Visitors whose preference was for cheaper, less palatial accommodation arrived in the Blue Mountains. In 1905 the local business community established the Katoomba and Leura Tourist Association which set about an energetic promotion of the two closely linked townships. By

Main Street, Katoomba, ca. 1890 between Katoomba and Park Streets where the photographer posed Hardy and Co's Superior Blue Mountains Coaches. (Springwood Hist. Soc.)

Main Street Katoomba ca. 1910 when gas light fittings stand in the street and cabbies are lined up waiting for the trains to arrive. Most of these buildings still stand in Main Street. (Blue Mts Hist. Soc.)

Tabrett's Mountain Coaching and Motoring Company serving the tourism boom was in the vicinity of Gearin's Hotel, opposite the railway crossing. Another Tabrett was well-known in Katoomba for his shoe place. (Blue Mts Hist. Soc.)

An ambling pedestrian and motor tour around the cliff's edge at Katoomba in 1907.
(Blue Mts City Lib.)

"Operating modern Tourist Cars to Jenolan Caves and all Mountain Sights daily. Accommodation arranged at all leading Guest Houses free of charge. Travel the Dind's way — for a Happy Holiday. No. 1 Booking Office, Central Buildings, opposite Railway Station, Katoomba, No. 2 Office, Waratah Street. 'Phone 415 Katoomba," was written beneath this touring vehicle. (Blue Mts Hist. Soc.)

the time World War I darkened the horizon Katoomba was entering its 'boom' period.

This 'boom', which peaked in the post-war optimism of the 1920s, saw numerous less expensive and smaller, though often multi-storeyed, guesthouses spring up all over Katoomba. Gradually it took on that distinctive congested appearance that sets it apart from the other Mountain towns where the holiday cottage seemed to predominate. By 1917 there were approximately sixty guesthouses operating in the town.

The motor car also revolutionised tourist activities. The leisurely pace of the old horse-drawn vehicles was replaced by the exhilaration of speed. First the open top 'tourers' and, later, the sleek, elongated motor coaches, accommodating groups of twenty people or more in weather-proofed comfort, made it possible for visitors to see more in the time at their disposal. The tourist coach firms flourished in most of the Mountain towns. Many of the guesthouses also kept their own private fleet of vehicles to service their guests. But the increasing capacity for speed and the gradual enclosure of the 'sightseers' exacted its price, reducing their contact with the landscape they travelled through.

The popularity of the old walking tracks declined as promotional emphasis was placed on passive enjoyment of the scenery and interest was redirected to the cliff tops where lookouts to popular views were improved. Much of this work was done during the Great Depression of the late 1920s and early 1930s, when all three local government authorities on the Mountains used the Unemployment Relief Scheme to improve and maintain tourist attractions. The Projecting Platform at Echo Point, and the Cliff Drive and Prince Henry Cliff walk (both linking the lookouts along the cliff between Leura and Katoomba) were all opened at this time.

To the holiday-makers and honeymooners who flocked to guesthouses during the twenties and thirties, Katoomba was the holiday capital of New South Wales. They spent their days touring the sights in their charabancs and putting 'roses in their cheeks' in the bracing mountain air. In the evenings they danced, roller-skated, or went to see the latest moving pictures.

Newlyweds made up a large proportion of the visiting population and established Katoomba's reputation as a honeymooner's retreat. 'Lovesickness' was in the mountain air. Local businessmen exploited romance in their advertising. The 'Honeymoon Express' roared in on its regular run from Sydney, and on the lighter side the local wags, who circulated humorous stories and jokes, argued that the town should change its name — this time to "Honeymooney"! During the 1920s and 1930s Katoomba was, indeed, the "Queen City of the Hills".

Katoomba Railway Crossing ca. 1924. The house in the far left occupied the site of the present Hotel Metropole (completed in 1932). It was probably built in the late 1870s and was the country residence of the Reverend Baber of St Thomas's Church, North Sydney. (Blue Mts Hist. Soc.)

Many professional guides operated from Katoomba taking visitors into the Megalong valley. A shooting party guided by Mr Bone, on its way from Katoomba to the Megalong valley. (Keith Duncan/Blue Mts City Lib.)

Mr Bone and female companion at campsite in the Megalong Valley. (Keith Duncan/Blue City Lib.)

"The Boys from the Western Plains"

When war broke out in August 1914, the towns on the Blue Mountains were caught up in a wave of patriotism and in the early months of the conflict the region contributed its fair share of men to the Empire's cause.

As the war progressed and news of the heavy casualties in the Dardanelles and France made people realise that it was likely to be a long and bloody affair, uncertainty disturbed public optimism. Before the war was twelve months old community leaders throughout the country were worried by the decline in enlistments.

"The Allies", said the editor of the *Blue Mountains Echo* on 13 August, 1915, "can make no further progress in the Dardanelles until reinforced with troops. Our own men there are calling for assistance."

The Coo-ee March, the first of several at this time, was organised in Gilgandra by local businessman, W.T. Hitchen, in response to the recruitment problem. As it wound its way through the central west of N.S.W., over the Blue Mountains and down to the Domain in Sydney, it fuelled patriotism in the towns it passed through and swelled its ranks accordingly. By the time the Coo-ees arrived in Sydney the original thirty Gilgandra recruits had grown to over two hundred and sixty.

The marchers passed over the Blue Mountains in November, 1915. Katoomba and other Mountain towns seized the opportunity to express their patriotism with dramatic and colourful welcomes.

On Friday, 5 November, a large crowd gathered at the Explorers' Tree to hear the Mayor, Alderman G. James, welcome "the boys from the Western Plains" who marched into Katoomba to the accompaniment of the Leura Brass band and the cheers of the locals from footpaths and balconies. Katoomba was "a blaze of brightly-coloured bunting; long streamers arched the principal thoroughfares,

"Gladiators with the eyes of children" — young soldiers pose for Harry Phillips in Katoomba.
(Blue Mts Hist. Soc.)

Katoomba. "No less than 21 recruits", reported the *Echo,* "offered, and were accepted."

The entry of the Coo-ees into Springwood on Monday morning, 8 November, was a colourful affair. They had been joined at Faulconbridge by an escort of four mounted policemen and a squad from the Springwood Rifle Club and as they swung into the town a group of children from the local public school attached itself to the procession. A piper added the final touch and the men from the West were paraded to camp with the accompaniment of stirring highland music.

In the cool shade of the turpentine trees that grew

The Coo-ees march from Gilgandra to the Domain picking up recruits on the way. Twenty-one recruits from Katoomba joined up after watching this colourful and spirited march through Main Street in 1915. (Blue Mts Hist. Soc.)

Harry Phillips, photographer extraordinaire, must have perched in a precarious spot to capture this unique image of the Coo-ees marching up Berghofer's Pass to Katoomba. There is evidence of camera shake. (Blue Mts Hist. Soc.)

and many public and private houses were gaily bedecked ... ."

That evening an official dinner was held at The California guesthouse and further speeches of loyalty and welcome were delivered. Alderman Tabrett, proposing the toast to "Our Boys at the Front", declared that "the whole world rung with the praises of the Austral heroes who were ably defending the liberty of the world." He told the Coo-ees: "We want thousands more like you ... I sincerely hope Australia will always be noted for its workers and not its shirkers." The recruiting rally which followed the dinner was one of the biggest meetings ever seen in

The marchers continued on through Springwood on 8 November, 1915 where they were joined by local schoolchildren, four mounted policemen, the local rifle club and a piper. (Blue Mts City Lib.)

around their camp site, the recruits were served a fine lunch prepared by the ladies of Springwood. During the afternoon a number adjourned to the School of Arts to write letters while others, preferring a more active leisure, volunteered to fight a bushfire burning in the vicinity of the town.

In the evening an open-air concert and recruiting meeting were held at the camp, with a thousand people attending and an number of young men joining up. The following morning at nine o'clock, with the piper again in attendance, the Coo-ees marched out of town and headed for Penrith.

The Katoomba Red Cross Comforts Fund presented the Coo-ees with "a bale of socks from the Katoomba Red Cross Society and other ladies and ten pairs of socks from Mrs G. James (Mayoress)" according to the Blue Mountains Echo on 12 November, 1915. The workers are seen here outside the St Elmo guesthouse accompanied by its proprietor Mrs Wootton, seated on the left in the dark dress. (Blue Mts. Hist. Soc.)

Harry Phillips

The Blue Mountains has featured in the work of numerous photographers. Names like Kerry, Kitch, Howell, Lowden, Fowler, Manning and Green all readily come to mind but perhaps the most popular, and certainly one of the most talented, was Harry Phillips.

In 1908 Phillips, an unemployed printing machinist suffering from an injury which had cost him his job, arrived in Katoomba to recuperate. After three weeks camping out with his wife and daughter the landscape had made such an impression that he decided to settle in the area permanently.

He fixed his affairs in Sydney and established a small photographic and confectionary business in Katoomba Street. He nurtured an interest in photography and much of his time was now spent experimenting with his camera at all the local vantage points.

As business expanded he combined his talent for photography with his skill as a printer, producing the Blue Mountains viewbooks for which he has become best known. These books reveal Phillips high production standards and flare for the dramatic presentation of his subjects. Titles like *Blue Mountains Wonderland, 81 Views* and *Views of the Far-Famed Blue Mountains* have become, in recent years, sought after collectors items.

Phillips loved the Blue Mountains with a passionate intensity that fuelled his life-long enthusiasm for promoting the region. A perfectionist, he would wait patiently for the perfect moment before taking a photograph and often risk his own safety in order to get the shot he wanted.

He worked hard at distribution and his viewbooks circulated widely. By 1919 100,000 copies of *Blue Mountains Wonderland* had been dispersed throughout Australia and overseas. Soldiers wrote to him from the trenches of World War I and copies

of his books were found in the German dugouts.

He experimented with promotional schemes. He suggested to the local council an exhibition on the Blue Mountains in San Francisco, a permanent display in Sydney, the building of a scenic railway and the operation of a scenic lift at Echo Point.

Personal profit was not his concern. He gave his viewbooks away generously and, much to the despair of his wife, insisted on keeping them at an unprofitable price. His preoccupation with developing his ideas and perfecting his product meant the practicalities of business and the running of his shop were left largely to his wife, Isabel. Mrs Phillips kept the books, ordered new stock and handled customer relations. While Phillips, the slightly built and formally attired enthusiast, was known and greeted around town as 'Harry', his wife was always a respectful 'Mrs Phillips' in recognition of her role in the family business.

Both the poet and the prophet were present in

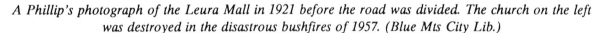

A Phillip's photograph of the Leura Mall in 1921 before the road was divided. The church on the left was destroyed in the disastrous bushfires of 1957. (Blue Mts City Lib.)

Harry Phillips with his wife Isabel Jane and their daughter Isabel May, 1918. (Blue Mts City Lib.)

Phillip's nature and nowhere is this more apparent than in his abiding fascination with clouds and mist. It was common, when a mist rose up from the Jamison Valley or an interesting formation of clouds appeared, to hear around town "Harry's happy". In fact, on such occasions he was known to race from his shop, spend the whole day 'in the clouds' and return late only to lock himself in his darkroom.

His interest in clouds and the constantly changing patterns in the sky above the Blue Mountains, led to the publication in 1914 of *The Cloud.* The book featured a series of cloud portraits illustrating Shelley's well-known poem. A central photograph was of a unique grouping of clouds he had seen above Katoomba in 1909.

A devoutly religious man, with a spiritual rather than dogmatic bent, Phillips turned this photograph into a very personal statement of belief. He titled it 'War Clouds' and interpreted in the formation a divine forecast of World War I. The photograph was published widely overseas and sent to many of the world's leaders. It caused a great deal of interest in the years prior to the war, bringing him a small degree of international recognition and involving him in considerable correspondence on the subject.

Another experience he described reveals the intensity of his work. It occurred "one beautiful morning, when visiting Narrow Neck, on the Blue Mountains, for the purpose of photographing clouds in the valleys. Suddenly a cloud rose out of the valley and for fully two minutes I stood spellbound. Before me, about 200 feet away, a figure stood upright, and encircling the head was a beautiful rainbow coloured halo. I had my camera under my arm, but my thoughts were too fully occupied with the realisation of the possibility of Christ having a halo round his head when on earth. Twice since, with others, I have seen our own shadows cast down into the valley of mist,

Govett's Leap Road, Blackheath, where three young ladies pose beneath a remarkable Mountain's cloud formation. (Blue Mts Hist. Soc.)

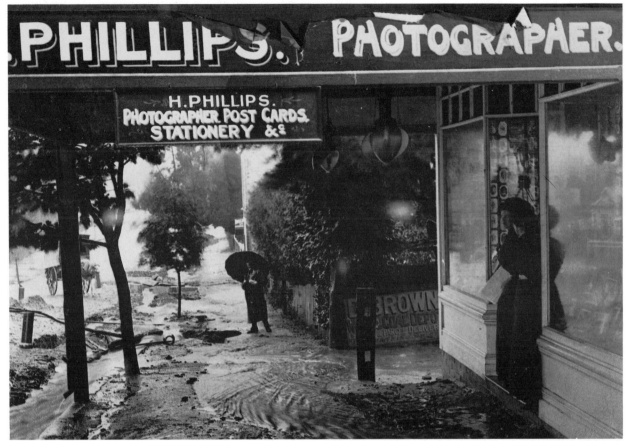

Typical Mountain weather outside Harry Phillips' first shop in Katoomba. Phillips lived and worked here in 1909. The building still stands today at 159 Katoomba Street. (Blue Mts City Lib.)

Phillips pursues his passion for photography up a tree in his own backyard in Katoomba, ca. 1918. (Blue Mts City Lib.)

with rainbows or halos round our heads, but these were not so convincingly clear as that first figure I had seen standing upright over the top of the Blue Mountains."

Perhaps the last word on Phillips and his photographic legacy should go to his biographer, Phillip Kay: "I have to thank Harry Phillips for teaching me more about the history of the area, and for showing me how to look at its natural beauties in a new way. Not only does he convey his love and commitment to his subject in these photographs, but he leaves one with a sense of fragility of all fine things. This awareness encourages us to preserve what could so easily be destroyed."

Mountain Guesthouses

In the 1880s accommodation was required by staff of the various schools, railway stations and services. Many widows found that keeping a boarder or two brought in a modest income. Until the depression in the 1890s the Blue Mountains towns flourished and many competent tradesmen and builders came to work on the erection of large and elegant hotels such as the Belgravia and the Palace (the Ritz) at Leura. The 1890s also saw the building of accommodation for middle and working class folk who could afford holidays in the Mountains. These hotels and houses became the location for thousands of honeymoons, and holidaymakers booked year after year. By 1921, at the height of the guesthouse era, there were at least a hundred accommodation houses in the Mountains.

Text and captions: Gwen Silvey

Above: John Britty North — known as the father of Katoomba — in 1876 opened up a coal mine near Katoomba Falls. Being the owner of much land around the area at the time, he and relative, Mrs Weynton, built several houses in Walgett Street on land running up to Bathurst Road. One of these, near the western end of Walgett Street, was used in those early days by Mrs Weynton's daughters as a boarding house named 'Shirley'. The Misses Weynton are shown (apparently in their "Sunday best") seated in the above photograph. It is said that the first Congregation Church services in Katoomba were held in Mrs Weynton's own home. 'Shirley', with its long front verandah is still extant as a private home in Walgett Street.(Blue Mts Hist. Soc.)

Left: Mrs Walter Rumble was a famous guesthouse proprietor in Katoomba — first conducting a homely weatherboard house named 'Sans Souci' in Lurline Street. Her business flourished, so she purchased a cottage on a large block of land in Lovel Street, and by 1917 the first section (pictured) of the new 'Sans Souci' had been erected there by local builder Hugh Milligan. The old boarding house in Lurline Street had changed its name and passed to other hands, and Mrs Rumble advertised her new establishment widely as providing unsurpassed panoramic views of the Blue Mountains. By 1924 she announced it had doubled in size after recent additions, offering every facility including four new lounges, a billiard room and tennis courts. 'Sans Souci' was one of the largest and most popular guesthouses on the Blue Mountains. It still dominates the skyline on the heights east of Katoomba Railway Station, having been used as a nursing home since 1960. (Blue Mts Hist. Soc.)

The only public house ever to be erected in Leura, Alexandra Hotel was named for the queen consort of the reigning King Edward VII when it opened for business in 1903. Situated on the heights between the Great Western Highway and Leura Railway Station the Alexandra, its balconies highly decorated with turned wood, was indeed fortunate to survive the disastrous fires which swept past it in 1957, and today remains the only licensed hotel in Leura. (Blue Mts Hist. Soc.)

The first 'Clarendon', built ca. 1884 was one of only four houses existing in Katoomba Street when the town was proclaimed a municipality in 1889. Located beside the Carrington Hotel, this boarding house was run in the 1880s by Mrs Simonson, a native of Tralee, wife of a builder, and mother of seven daughters — one of whom married the first schoolmaster at Katoomba, John Douglass. The establishment was later known as 'Clarendon House', and subsequent to its purchase by Sir James Joynton Smith (then the owner of the Carrington) it was refurbished, with Art Nouveau glazing to match that being added to the Hotel, for a private residence for his wife. In later years the building reverted to a rooming house, and sadly deteriorated before burning down. The block of three shops north of Katoomba Post Office were erected in front of 'The Clarendon' in the 1920s. (Blue Mts Hist. Soc.)

This house, built in 1913 as the residence of the Coulter family, was opened in 1921 as a guesthouse named 'Villers Bret' by Captain Gadd who had recently returned from service with the first A.I.F. in France. After a few years he appointed an experienced guesthouse proprietor, Miss Cameron, as manageress, but he retained ownership of the establishment until about 1940 when it became a novitiate for Roman Catholic nuns. Later on it was re-named 'Fern Tree Lodge' and served as a drug re-habilitation centre for the time prior to its demolition in 1985. The site, beside the Clarendon Motel, now forms part of the carpark from the R.S.L. Club. The photograph was taken in 1924 by Mr Eric Breedon, whose wife is seated at bottom right of the picture. (Blue Mts Hist. Soc.)

With its roof garden thirty metres long overlooking Katoomba Street and the valleys beyond, 'Hampton Villa' occupied a premier town site on the corner of Waratah Street for about sixty years. It was eventually demolished prior to the building of the Ford Sales and Service Station on that corner. In 1917 Mrs G. Birney advertised her establishment in flowery language, and said that accommodation was assured for over 200 people. (Blue Mts Hist. Soc.)

One of the very early boarding houses in Katoomba was 'Montrose'. Together with 'Glenample' next door, it was operated in the 1880s by Mrs W. Baird. Centrally situated in those days on Bathurst Road, only a few doors down towards the Railway Station from 'Balmoral House', 'Montrose' was a well known building until demolished in the early 1960s when the site was used to build a service station which in turn disappeared in 1990. When Mr and Mrs George Adams came to 'Montrose' from 'Mount View' in 1919 they soon decided to buy 'Balmoral House' which remained under their management from 1921 until their retirement many years later. Meanwhile 'Montrose' was advertised as a guesthouse until about 1925, and was let as a rooming house for its last years. (Blue Mts Hist. Soc.)

Braemar, Macquarie Road, Springwood

In Springwood, where few examples of the town's nineteenth century buildings remain, 'Braemar' provides a valuable link with the community's past. Built in 1892 for Sydney businessman, James Hunter Lawson, it is a fine though modest example of developing federation styles.

J. H. Lawson, a young nineteen-year-old cabinet-maker from Greenock in Scotland, arrived in Sydney in 1855. Apparently finding the local cabinet-making scene in a slump, he entered the hotel business for a number of years before eventually establishing his own furniture and cabinet-making firm in the early 1860s. By 1884 he was advertising his business as "Art

Pictured are James Hunter Lawson, standing, his son Alfred, with the horse, and in the carriage his wife Emma, daughter Flora and grandchildren Ethel, Emma and Ernest in front of 'Braemar'. (Blue Mts City Lib.)

Furniture Makers, Upholsterers and Carpet Warehousemen ... with special designs for furniture for Entrance Halls, Drawing Rooms, Dining Rooms and Libraries."

The business thrived and Lawson's sons (he had married Emma Glen of Pyrmont in 1857) were introduced into the business as they became old enough. A measure of his success can be seen in his purchase of twenty four hectares of land at Springwood in the fashionable Blue Mountains

where he began a building programme which saw the erection that year of both the Oriental Hotel and a small country house he named 'Braemar'. A year or two later, immediately adjacent to 'Braemar', he built a second home, 'Glen Lawson', which he and his wife occupied until their deaths in 1926.

First 'Braemar' and then 'Glen Lawson' became the country retreat of the large Lawson family — seven boys and two girls, their wives, husbands and the numerous grandchildren. Judging by surviving photographs James Hunter enjoyed playing the family patriarch, though his Turkish fez and the general hint of showmanship in his bearing attest to a less than autocratic approach to his role. His eldest son, James Robert, a regular visitor and well-known for his own theatricality of dress and manner, had also established himself in the world of business. In

1886 he founded a firm of auctioneers that became the forerunner of the business that still bears his name today.

When the Lawsons moved next door 'Braemar' was then let and, since the mid-1890s, has been used as a private dwelling, a convalescent hospital, a doctor's residence and surgery and, for many years from the 1920s onward, as a guesthouse. In 1973 'Braemar' was purchased by the Blue Mountains City Council and became the headquarters of the district's first public library. Following a period leased to the Prospect County Council as office space, the building was then restored as a Bicentennial project, its interior being adapted to house both a small art gallery and the public library's Local Studies Collection. Accessible to the public since 1988, the old building has found a useful role in Springwood's contemporary life.

J.H. Lawson with his grandchildren, Ernie and Ethel Urquhart, on Braemar's front steps. (Miss S.E. Lawson/Blue Mts City Lib.).

How Katoomba got its name

In his later years Harry Peckman attained the status of 'an old local identity' and was interviewed many times by the Mountains and city press. One of his favourite and often repeated stories concerned the origins of the name 'Katoomba'. Here is what he told a journalist from the *Blue Mountains Echo* in February, 1919:

"Somewhere in the seventies, James Neale erected the first house here. He was delighted with the scenery, and tried to learn the native name for the place. With this end in view he sought out Princess Betsy of the Kanimbla Tribe at Hartley, and brought her to Katoomba where she was entertained at a picnic. She informed him that he place was known as Katoomba, which meant 'Tumble-down-water'. And Katoomba it was thenceforth designated."

There seems no reason to doubt the authenticity of this story, as it was Peckman's, carriage which transported the party to their picnic near Katoomba Falls. The word 'Katoomba', however, may not be the most accurate rendering of the Aboriginal pronunciation. In other versions of the story it is written as 'Katumba' and the meaning given as 'all shiny falling waters'. Kedumba, as in Kedumba Pass, is probably a further variant of the same Aboriginal word. It is also worth noting that as early as 1833 Surveyor Govett recorded the Aboriginal place name, 'Go Doom Ga', at a point on the Cox's River now beneath the waters of Lake Burragorang.

When Princess Betsy died she was buried in the Kanimbla Valley. Peckman, who knew and admired her, wrote the following epitaph on her grave:

Where now the gum-tree sheds its leaves,
And the golden wattles bloom;
And the Goddess Flora softly weaves
A native wreath o'er Betsy's tomb.

Today, no trace of the grave or its inscription remains.

Katoomba Falls, Katoomba's name meaning "Tumble down water". (Blue Mts City Lib.)

"The enchanting idea of waterfalls"

When William Charles Wentworth was crossing the Blue Mountains in 1813 he remarked on "the moisture which the Mountains inhale from the clouds" and how this gave "rise to the innumerable small streams which everywhere pervade the Mountains." Water is a key factor in the ecology of the Blue Mountains. It is also of great historical and economic importance. Since the grandeur of the falls at the Weatherboard and Govett's Leap brightened an otherwise tedious journey for Charles Darwin in 1836, water has played a significant role in the tourist promotion of the area.

Wentworth Falls, a Mountain township named for its major waterfall, won early recognition "for the beauties of its watercourse and waterfalls." The *Blue Mountains Encyclopaedia,* a popular tourist guide of the mid-1920s, remarked that the town's "chief glory is its profusion of water. The very name of many of the more famous scenic beauties demonstrates this startling truth. Wentworth Falls, valley of the waters, Weeping Rock, Water Nymphs Dell, reveal the true nature of the town's garland of native beauty. Picturesque creeks purl over mossy rocks; countless tributaries converge from a myriad of shady dells, to create a rippling cascade that dashes onward to develop into a fall. Wherever one turns there is water — leaping, splashing, dashing, foaming, eddying, swirling — it careers down rocky beds, hurls itself over cliffs, makes a sober passage among mosses and ferns and otherwise disports itself as only the clear, limpid, saltless Blue Mountains streamlets can."

The beauty of the region's waterfalls was extolled with great enthusiasm in early tourist literature and the photographic images of numerous falls, many largely forgotten today, circulated widely as popular subjects of postcard series. With titles like Weeping Rock and The Bridal Veil such images stirred the imagination and carried with them wherever they were sent something of the romance and poetry of

The White family in the Valley of the Waters, ca. 1912. (Mrs D. Kirk/Blue Mts City Lib.)

Pretty Linda Falls at Leura.
(Mrs D. Kirk/Blue Mts City Lib.)

the Blue Mountains. As symbols of the region, many waterfalls became as well-known internationally as the Three Sisters are today.

Water and waterfalls have always been an important part of people's personal experience of the Blue Mountains. There is something timeless about the flow of water, something that speaks deeply to the reflective side of human nature. Towards the end of her life the novelist, Kylie Tennant, remembered "the most beautiful waterfalls" as one of her earliest and most cherished childhood memories of the Blue Mountains.

Now, I have always been interested in water. I love to see it falling into pools, I love fresh water. Fresh water is one of the things that has been very important in my life. (When) we came for a holiday to the Blue Mountains ... I was able to wallow in little pools with gold sand ringed round them and see ferns and waterfalls ... the enchanting idea of waterfalls was my earliest association with the Blue Mountains.

These leisurely old walks

In the early years of the tourist industry the principal recreational interest was the active enjoyment of walking. A well-established system of tracks, constructed mainly by members of the early, local 'reserves trusts', and often beginning with steps hewn out of a sheer cliff face, drew the visitor down from the popular lookouts and into the valleys with their waterfalls and cool ferny hollows.

Soberly attired and armed with stout walking sticks and plenty of time, visitors explored the bush in a quiet and leisurely manner. The provision of ladders, railings, walkways, seats and picnic tables, all hewn from rough bush timber enhanced their enjoyment. "These leisurely old walks", comments local historian Jim Smith, "were beautifully designed to blend in with the landscape. Many of them are masterpieces of landscape art."

As mining enterprises halted, tracks and other vantage points which had been opened during the course of operations were converted to recreational use and increased the options for walkers. Popularity of the walking tracks reached a peak during the decade prior to World War I, in the years before the automobile changed the recreational habits of visitors.

Despite the advent of the motor car, some tracks remained popular. The federal Pass was opened in 1900 but continued to be well patronised into the 1920s and received a further boost to its popularity with the opening of the Giant Stairway and the Scenic Railway in the early 1930s.

The photographer, Harry Phillips, a promoter of local attractions, gave many of the local walks considerable space in his publications. Here is how, in his own inimitable style, he invites his readers to enjoy the Federal Pass in his *The Blue Mountains & Jenolan Caves Illustrated Tourist Guide,* published in the 1920s:

The Pass is entered from the Leura side a few hundred yards beyond the Leura Cascades, through fern clad walks, round torturous mountain paths,

The agonies of holidaying as suffered by this Sydney family. Sydney Mail 26 February 1896. (Mitchell Lib.)

sweeping into fairy dells and avenues of huge eucalyptus, topped with matted growths of wild clematis. From a point in the Pass a glorious glimpse of the Bridal Veil is obtained through the trees. Onward through heavy-foliaged forests, past hung walls of Nature's masonry, over rustic bridges spanning tiny rivulets, under giant tree-ferns, through fragrant jungle, the path continues. Hopetoun Bower is one of the features of the Pass. Some distance further the path begins to ascend, going underneath the Three Sisters which stands out in bold relief. At the half-way resting place the traveller has a glorious view of the Jamison Valley, while immediately behind are immense walls of rock, and standing sentinel-like in the distance is Mount Solitary. The track now doubles round the Three Sisters and leads to Katoomba. For half-a-mile it passes through sombre-timbered country, and then for another mile, up and down, in and out, through sylvan glades, forest palaces, over stony bridges and rustic stairs, across bubbling water and water-formed excavations right up to the last falls at Katoomba, where the Pass ends and the ascent of the cliffs commences.

It was not only in the upper Blue Mountains that walkers found pleasure in wandering bush pathways. The lower Mountains had their popular walks and well-patronised picnic spots. One of the most popular of these was Sassafras Gully, sometimes known as Flying Fox Gully, at Springwood. Still popular today, this area was dedicated as a Reserve for Public Recreation in 1888 and featured prominently in all the early tourist publications. In the 1882 edition of the Gibbs & Shallard *Pictorial Guide to the Blue Mountains of New South Wales* it is described as follows:

> In a walk of ten minutes along a well-defined track, at the back of the residence of Mr J.B. Hoare, with marked trees to guide him, the tourist will arrive at the head of a deep and rocky gully, shaded on all sides by huge honeycombed overhanging rocks,

The White Family have many photographic recollections of happy outings on bush trails. (Mrs D Kirk/Blue Mts City Lib.)

covered with large sassafras, myrtle, turpentine and other trees, interlaced and bound together with supplejacks and other robust climbing and twining plants. A stream of clear water runs into and overflows a chain of ponds about a mile down this gully; and the sides of the creek are clothed with a dense covering of ferns and mosses. The stem of the trees are green with this moist luxuriant growth, and botanists declare that for beauty, and number, and rarity of varieties of ferns and allied vegetation, this district equals any known.

The track to Linda Falls was partly furnished with hand made stairs, bridges and sapling rails. (Mrs D. Kirk/Blue Mts City Lib.)

National Pass. (Blue Mts Hist. Soc.)

Mountain Air

A 1980s tourist slogan used to promote the Blue Mountains urged people to "Come Up For Air!", a modern expression of a longstanding belief in the vitalising and restorative qualities of Mountain air. Folk wisdom viewed living in the Blue Mountains as a guarantee of good health and long life.

"You have no idea what a salubrious region this is," the young heroes of Thomas Knox's fictional travelogue, *The Boy Travellers in Australasia* (1889), were told as their train climbed into the Blue Mountains. "The air is wonderfully bracing, so much so that it is a common saying, 'Nobody ever dies in the Blue Mountains unless he is killed by accident or blown away'."

From the 1870s the smell of sewage was an unbearable part of hot Sydney summers and the wind was thought to carry disease. The cooler climate and cleaner air of the Blue Mountains was an attractive lure to citizens of the metropolis. "To those debilitated by strenuous work in the cities", the *Katoomba Daily* declared in 1920, "or suffering with any form of anaemia, nerves or lassitude, a course of the ozone-laden winds proves a veritable elixir of life."

The authority of science was used to bolster popular belief. The medical philosophy of Dr Phillip E. Muskett, an authority on "the feeding and management of Australian infants", was featured in numerous editions of *The Mountaineer Pocket Tourist Guide,* one of the most popular early guides to the Blue Mountains. Dr Muskett advised his readers that:

> Mountain air is more rarefied than ordinary air. It is perfectly pure also, and free from all atmospheric dust and micro-organisms.

> Mountain air contains a relatively large amount of ozone. Ozone itself being one of the most powerful disinfectants known, it follows that it is a greater purifier of the air — and, further, ozonised air is healthy and stimulating. ... with most people Mountain air acts as a general tonic, and promotes

Invigorating mountain air stimulates the appetite for a lunchtime picnic on the rocky ridges, n.d. (John Falloon, Blue Mts City Lib.)

the appetite. Not only do they eat well, but usually sleep well too. Indeed, it generally acts especially on literary and professional men as a soporific. The rest, too, is very much more refreshing than that obtained at lower levels — six hours sleep being as good as eight hours elsewhere. Mountain air has, further, the remarkable property of promoting metabolism ... In this way it replaces the worn-out tissues with new material.

Tuberculosis sufferers flocked to the sanitariums, assured of the special value of the pure, dry, rarefied mountain air. The Katoomba and Leura Tourist Association declared, in their 1905 guidebook, that "there has never been a case of consumption among the permanent inhabitants." Those with lesser complaints sought out the guesthouses and holiday cottages, all eager to endure a dose of stoic exposure to "the keen biting winds of the Mountains". The region seemed to offer the possibilities of a Shangri-la and the local business community loved it.

Everybody in the Mountains knew somebody who had turned one hundred. Our young "Boy Travellers", mentioned earlier, were given "an authentic account of a man who celebrated his one hundred and first birthday. The man used to speak of a neighbour who lived to be one hundred and eight years old and hadn't an unsound tooth in his head, when he was killed by the kick of a vicious horse."

Perhaps the humorists should have the last word to say on the subject of Mountain air. The following story was published in the *Blue Mountains Echo* in April, 1920:

Healthy on the Mountains — Rather! Why, a Sydney visitor began to talk to an old man outside a cottage in Station Street, the other day, and asked him his age. Said the Katoomba ancient, 'I am just over 70.' 'Well,' said the visitor, 'you look as if you have a good many years to go yet. At what age did your father die?' 'Father dead?' said the oldster, looking surprised. 'Father ain't dead — he's inside putting grandfather to bed'.

In reference to the effects of mountain air, the Blue Mountains Gazette *wrote on 5 June, 1903 in its Women's Column to readers. "... if they really knew how beneficial mountain mists are to the skin, we would see more young ladies taking advantage of a misty day for an outing. The dry climate of Australia causes the skin to become dried in appearance. The mist or moisture of the atmosphere is necessary for the production of the blooming cheeks. What better then than a real heavy mist that sinks into the skin and softens it? Girls, you have the very thing right at your doors; why not take advantage of it?" (Photo Harry Phillips/Blue Mts Hist. Soc.)*

The Paragon Sundae and Candy Store, ca. 1925. (Blue Mts. City Lib.)

A Paragon of service and style

The Paragon Cafe was the dream of Zacharias Simos who arrived in Australia from Greece early this century. His disembarked in Sydney and lined up on the wharf with other immigrants where Greek fish shop and cafe owners selected likely young men to work in their establishments. But Zacharias had plans of his own. He worked long and hard at several jobs, including door to door selling, until he had saved enough to start his own business in Katoomba Street. That was in 1916 when Katoomba was a booming tourist resort and a mecca for honeymooners.

The original tea room was designed in the classical tradition and in the mid-1930s two dining rooms were added: the Banquet Hall and the Blue Room, designed in the Art Deco style by Henry White who was also the architect for the State Theatre in Market Street, Sydney. One of The Paragon's interior features is the solid maple wall panelling on which is superimposed alabaster figures from Greek mythology. The soda fountain and milk bar, built between the wars, are among the few surviving in their original condition. Even the packaging and display of The Paragon's celebrated chocolates reflect those pre-war years.

When Zacharias Simos died, his wife continued to provide a standard of service in keeping with the name the establishment. Mrs Simos' own Greek background was far from traditional for that era. She grew up in Baltimore, USA, one of three children and the family returned to Greece when she was seven. It was a time, she says, 'when not many women had the opportunity to go to High School,' but her father insisted on their education. Her sister eventually became a stockbroker in New York and her brother was the head of Social Security in Greece. Her own son is a Q.C. educated at Cambridge and Harvard.

Mrs Simos has been a tireless worker for charity in Katoomba and continued managing The Paragon well into her eighties where she received visits from celebrities in all walks of life. She has also seen the building classified by the National Trust but perhaps more important is the nostalgic place the establishment holds in the hearts of so many Australians, a tradition that will continue in the years to come for no visit to Katoomba is complete without dropping in on the Paragon.

Cinemas — Saturday night at the pictures

Long before the arrival of television, 'going to the pictures' for both locals and visitors, had become a weekly ritual in the Blue Mountains. Blackheath had its Arcadia (later The Victory), Leura its Liberty, and Springwood its Roxy.

In Katoomba The Empire and The Kings were operating before World War I, the former advertising itself in 1909 as "the most up-to-date and best appointed Picture Theatre in the State". Both survived into the 1930s when The Kings was demolished and replaced by The Savoy (1936) and The Empire underwent an extensive revamp, striking back in 1937 as The Embassy.

All the great stars — cowboys and buccaneers, beauties and beasts — have strutted their stuff across the screens of the Mountain cinemas and many a fan has walked a long way, in all weathers, to see his or her favourite heroes and heroines.

One such fan was 'Joe' Makin who, as a youth in the 1920s, would walk from Leura to Katoomba to see the latest films on offer:

> Saturday night was one of my greatest nights when I was young, to get up and have a look at a picture show. Tom Mix, Buck Jones, Fred Thomson — the cowboy pictures were my favourites. I also remember one of Eddie Cantor's, 'The Hottentot' I think. I went and saw that twice, it was a terrific picture comedy.
>
> My eldest brother went up to see Ken Maynard in another cowboy picture. He came home and was talking about it, about how he tricked the Indians and so on, and I thought well, I've got to go and have a look at this.
>
> I used to walk. I hardly ever caught a bus, and I'd got up near St Mary's College when I heard this voice behind me saying 'Where are you going?' I looked around and it was a girl I knew. I said, 'What's the matter?' and she replied, 'I want to go up and see the picture and I've got this far but I'm wet.' It had come down this fine, wet, misty rain. Well, I thought,

The Savoy was built on the site of the Kings Theatre in the fashionable Art Deco style of the 1930s. It closed in 1975 (Blue Mts City Lib.)

The Embassy Katoo...

I can accomplish this alright and I took my coat off and put if over her and away we went to see the picture.

Well, I got interested in the picture and it came to this part where he was about to get this Indian and she got a bit excited and flung her arms up and caught me right on the side of the ear. Gee it stung. Anyway, it come interval and we went over to the shop opposite where she had a creaming soda and I had a lemonade.

Before the next picture they showed part of 'Felix the Cat'. It was the first time I'd seen animation. Well, I was holding her down in the seat half the time. Felix really got up to some tricks. The other picture started off and one of the songs in it was one of the old-time dance songs — 'Down the Shady Lane', I think, and there she was humming along with the song. I said, 'Quiet, people will get sick of this', but no way could you stop her. She was really interested in the picture.

Well, we come out of the show. 'We'll go in over here', I said, 'and have a cup of tea and toast.' So in we went — and then I realised I had three miles to walk instead of a mile and a half. I had to take her home. She wore my coat all the way. We walked across North Katoomba and down through the bush to her home. I got home at about a quarter to three in the morning. I thought, 'No more of this, I'm not having this on again!' It's amazing how these things happen.

As with many cinemas, the Kings Theatre was also used as a roller skating rink in the late 1920s before it was demolished to make way for the Savoy. This flashlight photograph was taken by A. Manning on 13 July 1929. (Blue Mts City Lib.)

The old Embassy Theatre was situated in Katoomba Street where Coles is today.(Wallace Green/Blue Mts City Lib.)

Auld Lang Syne

For many years the town of Katoomba was synonymous with the exhilaration of New Year's Eve celebration. The peak period occurred in the 1930s when Sydneysiders, who now crowd The Rocks or fall into the fountain at King's Cross, would arrive in their thousands to swell the local population.

It takes little coaxing for older residents to enthuse, with fond and vivid memories, about the times they kicked up their heels in the streets of Katoomba while welcoming in the new year. One such is George Mitchell, a former tourist coach driver, who remembers with real pleasure the joy and excitement that he and other revellers experienced. The high point of the night was undoubtedly the grand New Year's Eve parade.

On New Year's Eve for as far back as I can remember they had their procession. All traffic was closed off at Waratah Street. The procession used to start from Lurline Street where the R.S.L. is now and there would be a continual stream of floats going up. There was a judging box in the centre of Katoomba Street — in the junction of Katoomba and Main Streets — and after they had passed the judges they would go on around and back down to the R.S.L. Hall via Parke Street.

That would take about two hours I suppose, but the floats were terrific. I've seen the Chinese dragons where the legs were made up from the guests of just one guesthouse — the one I can remember particularly was from the Milroy. There were some weird and wonderful floats. Why it all failed I don't know!

Every New Year's Eve early in the morning, and even a couple of days before, different people with cars or trucks would be arranging everything for the parade. People wore costumes and horses were all done up. The business people — the milkmen, the bakers — their carts were all decorated and the horses. They had some beautiful horses — Clydesdales and so on. And all the balconies on the old shops in Katoomba Street — they were all packed with spectators.

Guests at Balmoral House on 31 December, 1936. Mr Adams, dressed as the policeman, was the proprietor and used to lead the parade. (Marion Brodrick, Blue Mts City Lib.)

Dave Brown as a bathing beauty, 1920s.
(Mrs Trixie Brown)

On top of the hill near the Carrington, where the bus stop is now, they had a big platform and it was run by comperes from 2KA and various places and they'd have community singing there. They used to give prizes for solos — they used to come up out of the audience. Quiz questions and all that — they really made it a big night.

At midnight the trains that were in the station would all blow their horns and everybody would join arms and start singing 'Auld Lang Syne'. It was really terrific. I wish those days were here now. It was a night we used to look forward to every year even when I was a kid.

Everybody came here — they came from miles away just to have a good time, it was a good night. Never any trouble for the police — they were well behaved crowds. They all had a good time. That's one part of Katoomba that I miss!

Katoomba Amusement Company

This company was formed in December 1911 to supply quality indoor, evening and holiday entertainment. The building was on the corner of Katoomba and Main Street, opposite the 'Carrington'. It showed daily matinees in the Photo Play Theatre and depicted "the latest and best the market produces in Drama, Science, Topical, Educational and the ever-necessary Comic." It seated 1000 people, had a skating rink operating three times daily to the strains of a ladies' orchestra. An additional attraction was a promenade on the Roof Garden, with its glassed arbor where patrons could enjoy the beautiful mountain scenery. World visitors included Harley Davidson (Champion Skater of the World) and Joe Munch (American Champion Skater). Their ads declared "Nothing that brains and money can devise has been overlooked."

The amusing staff of the Katoomba Amusement Company, ca. 1912, photographed by Harry Phillips. The company included a manager, secretary, assistant manager, musical director, chief operator and chief engineer, conductress of the ladies' orchestra, a rink instructor, and head skating mechanic, a skating rink ticket clerk and theatre ticket clerk. (Blue Mts Hist. Soc.)

Dave Ferguson's smithy yard at Springwood, ca. 1900. Blacksmiths were an important part of the community when the horse was the principal mode of transport. (Springwood Hist. Soc.)

Commerce

With the opening of the Western railway the Blue Mountains experienced an influx of population that resulted in the growth of permanent townships around the new railway platforms.

To meet the needs of these growing communities a commercial sector of retail shops, skilled tradesmen and other business enterprises emerged. Alongside schools, churches and courthouses appeared a vast array of services including butchers, bakers, dairymen, blacksmiths, real estate agents, bankers and the large 'Universal Providers'.

For the fashion conscious Mountain resident drapers provided the latest in millinery, gowns and blouses, and tailors fitted and styled in the latest patterns. Pharmacies offered large stocks of the latest drugs, patent medicines and toiletries. Carriers carted wood and coal and moved everything from pianos to luggage. There were painters and paperhangers, corset and abdominal belt makers, photographers and plumbers. Dentists filled teeth with gold, platinum and porcelin and 'painlessly' extracted the irrepairable. Hardware, ironmongery, boots and shoes, groceries, confectionery and stationery were all available, sometimes under the one roof of a large general store.

In a very short time there were few residents of the Blue Mountains who were out of reach of all the necessary and not so necessary, goods and services they required.

A butchering house, possibly located at the shale mining settlement at Nellies Glen in the Megalong Valley, ca. 1890. (Blue Mts Hist. Soc.)

Colliers Store on the corner of Bathurst Road and Govetts Leap Road, Blackheath in 1890. Colliers Central Store virtually supplied everything. (Jean Caldwell/Blue Mts City Lib.)

Christmas Eve, 1904, and the construction of the Tabrett Building in Katoomba Street, photographed by Kitch and Co. (Keith Duncan/Blue Mts City Lib.)

Butchers' carts outside the Wentworth Falls premises of James Bros. butchery. Nick Delaney, originally a storekeeper at Mount victoria in the 1880s, soon had businesses in villages as far afield as Wentworth Falls, and operated various baker's and cutting carts throughout the mountains. (Blue Mts Hist. Soc.)

Macquarie Road, Springwood, ca. 1915, showing the Emporium which sold drapery, shoes, crockery, enamel ware, stationery, tobacco and fancy goods, next door to the Frazer Memorial Church. (Springwood Hist. Soc.)

BELOW: The serving counter at Shaw's Butchers in Katoomba in the 1930s. (Miss M. Fawcett/Blue Mts City Lib.)

ABOVE: Dave Brown operated from a building in Park Street. They were a furniture removalists, packers and storers, and wood-and-coal merchants. (Trixie Brown/Blue Mts City Lib.)

Everett's store, ca. 1920s, in the Mullany and Co's premises in Main Street, Katoomba. The universal providers supplied quick deliveries to every part of the mountains. (Blue Mts Hist. Soc.)

*This interior is of the Men's Clothing section of Hendersons,
which was previously Mullanys third store in Main Street,
Katoomba, ca. 1920s. (Blue Mts Hist. Soc.)*

From Coal Mine to Scenic Railway

The decision to build a railway across the Blue Mountains in the late 1860s revived interest in the region's coal and shale resources, the importance of which had been noted as early as 1841 by the geologist, Rev. W. B. Clarke. In the 1860s Campbell Mitchell and Thomas Sutcliffe Mort established The Glen Shale Mine and began extracting kerosene shale from the Megalong Valley side of Narrow Neck Peninsula.

The coal and shale deposits of the adjoining Jamison Valley were left to the enterprise of John Britty North who registered his first company, The Katoomba Coal Mine, in 1878. He concentrated initially on working the coal seams outcropping on the eastern side of Narrow Neck near the Orphan Rock before undertaking extensive exploration of the Ruined Castle region in the early 1880s. Here he located profitable seams of kerosene shale and formed a second company, The Katoomba Coal and Shale Company, in 1885.

In 1882 North set up a loading platform at North's Siding on the main western railway line and constructed a tramway system that linked this facility with his mine in the valley. With the opening of his Ruined Castle enterprise he set about planning an elevated tramway, a flying fox to span the Jamison Valley from the company's Engine Bank near Katoomba Falls to the Ruined Castle ridge. Despite his importation of German engineers a fault found its way into the construction and, after carrying only 500 tonnes of shale, the whole system collapsed into the valley. Bushwalkers are still finding traces of it on their rambles.

The disaster spelled the end of North's company. In 1890 The Australian Kerosene Oil and Mineral Company entered the scene. It purchased the Glen Shale Mine and in 1891, obtained the remnants of North's activities at Ruined Castle and Orphan Rock. An extensive re-vamping of operations took place,

The Incline, now the Scenic Railway, c. 1887 when it was a tramway system for carrying shale out of the Jamison Valley. Its career changed when walkers began requesting lifts in the coal skip in the 1920s. (Photographed by John Paine/Macleay Museum)

with a tunnel being dug through Narrow Neck to link activities in the Megalong and Jamison Valleys. A horse tramway was constructed below the eastern ramparts of Narrow Neck, linking the Ruined Castle mines with both the new 'Daylight Tunnel' and the skipway leading to the cliff-top and North's Siding.

During the 1880s and 1890s the concentration of mine employees close to their work sites resulted in the appearance of several flourishing miners' villages. At South Katoomba, near the Falls, there was a hotel and several streets of weatherboard cottages. When the mines closed many of these were moved into the main part of Katoomba.

There was a substantial settlement at the bottom of Nellie's Glen in the Megalong Valley where a hotel, butcher's shop, bakery and public hall were all in evidence. At the Ruined Castle, the miners' accommodation was much rougher, occupied mainly by single men whose dwellings were fashioned from bush timber, kerosene tins or whatever material was at hand.

To the increasing numbers of wealthy, educated visitors arriving in Katoomba at this time, these primitive mining settlements were recommended as a 'picturesque' sidelight to an inspection tour of an unusual mining enterprise. "A visit to a coal mine would, at first sight appear somewhat prosaic", stated an early Railway Guide (1889), "but that at Katoomba is unlike any other of its class in Australia, by reason of its unique position and surroundings ... ."

As the nineteenth century drew to a close, mining activities went into decline. The seams of coal and shale were almost exhausted and uneconomic to mine. By 1903 coal and shale mining in the vicinity of Katoomba had ceased and the mining settlements broke up.

In 1925 a slight revival in the industry occurred when a local syndicate formed the Katoomba Colliery Ltd. and re-opened North's mine below the cliffs at South Katoomba. The old workings initially supplied a good deal of coal, much of which was sold to the Katoomba Powerhouse which supplied the town's electricity.

The Centennial, in South Katoomba in September, 1895. This was the miners' hotel and the scene of many a miners' altercation including one in February 1890 when a Swede named Anderson went berserk with a dagger assailing the publican and stabbing one Harry Simpson through the hand. As there was no court of Petty Sessions or lockup in Katoomba, he was conveyed by rail to the lockup in Penrith. (Blue Mts Hist. Soc.)

In the course of the mine's rehabilitation its haulage system at the Engine Bank incline opposite Orphan Rock was restored and when the mine began to experience difficulties in the 1930s the company sought to augment its declining income by providing visitors with rides in the empty coal skips. Little did they realise how significant this adaption was to prove!

Evidence suggests that transportation of visitors began in the 1920s when people walking the popular Federal Pass arrived at the mine and, rather than face a long, tiring climb up the steps at Katoomba Falls, they requested a lift in the coal skip. They were usually accommodated and made the journey up the incline

From the 1930s the Scenic Railway was an essential attraction for tourists visiting the mountains. (Blue Mts City Lib.)

kneeling on empty chaff bags spread on the floor of the truck.

In 1933 the mine management recognised the financial possibilities of their haulage skipway by officially launching the Katoomba Colliery Scenic Electric Cable Railway. It proved so popular that the number of public trips increased and eventually the company had a special passenger skip built which they named 'The Mountain Devil'. Sixpence got you a trip each way and the mine blacksmith, Fred Gull, appointed official guide by the colliery, would point out all the scenic attractions and describe the workings of the mine.

Mrs Grace Bayley, in a letter to the *Blue Mountains Gazette* on the occasion of the railway's fiftieth birthday, remembered a trip she took as a child in 1934:

> My mum and dad sat in the truck and my sister and I stood on the wooden rail at the back, hanging on to the back of the truck.
>
> The driver, whom I suppose was a miner, rode on the side and warned us to duck as we passed under the low roof when the rail takes its terrifying dip down the mountain.
>
> We were so excited it took a few seconds for his instruction to sink in and only just got down in time.
>
> Once at the bottom we had a look at the mine which was still working and saw one of the blind pit-ponies hauling coal out of the tunnel.
>
> The ride on the railway, although still a great experience, will never match that first thrill.

The Devil's 'conductor' was adept at his spiel and never failed to include a moment on the mine's declining fortunes and the increasing difficulty the miners were experiencing in making ends meet. At the end of the year there were smiles all round when Christmas presents, purchased with money collected by Mr Gull, were handed out to the children of the mining families.

When the Katoomba Colliery finally went into liquidation at the outbreak of World War II most of the plant and tracks were removed from the area. The exception was the equipment associated with the scenic cable railway.

The Three Sisters & Orphan Rock

Dramatic and awesome sensations are to be had riding on the Scenic Skyway which was installed in 1957 by Harry Hammon, the then and present owner. (Blue Mts City Lib.)

Two of the most widely recognised landforms of the Blue Mountains are Orphan Rock and The Three Sisters at Katoomba. They have been seen by millions throughout the world on postcards and in tourist brochures and travel books.

Orphan Rock, "standing solitary like a sentinel on duty", was most acclaimed by the nineteenth century tourist promoters. In the guidebooks it was commended as one of the major Katoomba sights, its close proximity to the Katoomba Coal Mine and Katoomba Falls focusing early attention on that part of South Katoomba.

The Three Sisters, on the other hand, marked as Triaxa Point on early maps, received comparatively little attention, evoking a degree of puzzlement in those who sought to describe them: "a cathedral with three spires" or "weird monuments of Egyptian architecture".

In the first decade of the twentieth century The Three Sisters gradually increased in prominence in promotional literature. In 1907 the N.S.W. Railways issued a guide to "picturesque resorts" in which the Carrington Hotel, exclusive and expensive, was linked with photographs of Orphan Rock and Katoomba Falls. By comparison, the less select but "cosy accommodation" of the Clarendon House boarding establishment was placed against the image of The Three Sisters.

In 1912 The Three Sisters appeared on the cover of the Katoomba Municipal Council's 'Official Tourist Guide' and the photographer Harry Phillips raised them in his work to almost mystical status. With the increasing popularity of Echo Point, enhanced in the 1930s by the construction of the Giant Stairway and the Projecting Platform lookout, The Three Sisters became established as the principal image of the Blue Mountains. Today they are, without question, the trademark of the region.

Enter Harry Hammon the current owner. In 1945, as a young man operating a transport business in Katoomba, he was at the site collecting a load of coal. It was a public holiday and nobody was around. Suddenly, a busload of Americans arrived and on finding the railway closed, loudly expressed their disappointment.

"I figured that if a bunch of Americans were interested enough to come right up from Sydney, and charter a bus into the bargain, the railway must have something", Hammon reminisced in 1983. He made a successful offer to buy the railway, installing in 1957, as a supplementary attraction, the first passenger-carrying horizontal cableway in the Southern Hemisphere — The Scenic Skyway.

Few visitors to the Blue Mountains leave without paying a visit to the Hammon complex at South Katoomba. Wise tourists use the railway, as a thrilling start or conclusion to a quiet bushwalk along one of the Jamison Valley tracks.

Orphan Rock, while overtaken in the popularity ratings, did retain its symbolic affiliations with exclusiveness and quality. For example, local alderman and businessman Charles Dash produced advertisements showing his flag planted firmly on its summit. "The Orphan Rock and Dash's Stand Alone", he proclaimed! Today it is the proprietors of The Paragon Cafe who maintains this tradition. For them Orphan Rock remains the hallmark of excellence.

Harry Phillip's Three Sisters. (Blue Mts Hist. Soc.)

Charles Dash's advertisement for his general store in Leura Mall. (Blue Mts City Lib.)

THE ORPHAN ROCK AND DASH'S STAND ALONE

Echo Point Memories:
The photographer, Mr Evans, was known as 'The Felix Man'. He posed people with Felix the Cat, Mickey Mouse and The Mountain Devil. The Mountain Devil was the name of the Scenic Railway's carriage and the dolls which took on the name were made from Lambertia formosa seeds and pipe cleaners and sold to tourists. Here left to right are: May Low on the right with Felix and friend in the 1930s, Pat Hinchliffe, nee Siggs, Terry Rigby and Robin Slade with the Mountain Devil, Christmas 1941. (John Low/Pat Hinchliffe/Colin Slade)

This Catalina was a R.A.A.F. plane dismantled and transported to Katoomba, re-assembled and placed on the artificial lake. All this was the brainchild of Mr Horace Gates, proprietor of Homesdale and Wentworth Cabaret. Tourists were rowed out by boat to the plane. Inside a film was shown simulating flying while outside a small speed boat circled, creating rocking waves. (Photo taken in 1946 and owned by Mr Lloyd Hughes.)

The Giant Stairway. (Blue Mts Hist. Soc.)

The Giant Stairway, Katoomba

On the afternoon of Saturday, 1 October, 1932, a stream of pedestrian and motorised traffic flowed down through Katoomba's streets to the cliff edge at Echo Point. The crowd had come to witness the official opening of the Giant Stairway and the modern projecting platform lookout.

At 3.30 p.m. the clouds, which had been dark and heavy with the hint of rain all morning, parted. The sun shone as the Premier of N.S.W., the Hon. B.S.B. Stevens, paid tribute to "the skill of the operatives who courageously carved out the Giant Stairway from the mountain side. They will always have the satisfaction of knowing that their initiative and labour will bring pleasure to countless thousands in the years to come." (*Katoomba Daily,* 4 October 1932)

The idea of a Giant Stairway linking Echo Point with the Federal Pass had been conceived some twenty years earlier by municipal ranger, James McKay. McKay was first employed in the early years of the century, soon after the opening of the Federal Pass (1900). Enthusiastic, dedicated and possessed of vision, he suggested in 1914 that a stairway down beside The Three Sisters was possible.

Katoomba Council approved the idea in 1916 and a start was made. After proceeding for almost a quarter of the distance, the hazardous and difficult job of hacking the steps out of the cliff face was deemed too costly and the project was brought to a halt. The whole idea then lapsed for over a decade.

In the early 1930s, as the depression worsened, the potential contribution of tourism to economic recovery was widely discussed. In the Blue Mountains such discussion encouraged a re-awakening of interest in schemes like the Giant Stairway and a decision to resume work on the project and to construct a new projecting platform lookout at Echo Point was passed through Council early in 1932. James McKay again took charge of operations and completed his task by the end of

Projecting Platform. (Blue Mts City Lib.)

September. "For people like myself", the Premier was heard to remark at the official opening, "who are not built for scaling precipitous cliffs, the Stairway offers a safe and comparatively easy way of enjoying the thrills of mountain-climbing without the attendant dangers of the pastime." (*Katoomba Daily*, 4 October 1932)

An eager crowd turned out for the opening of the Giant Stairway and Projecting Platform at Echo Point on Saturday October 1, 1932. The general public were assured that the projecting platform which came out two metres from the cliff edge "is so designed as to be absolutely safe, even when the platform is crowded to full capacity." (Harry Phillips/ Blue Mts City Lib.)

An injured walker being brought up the Giant Stairway in the 1940s. (Mrs V. Davis/Blue Mts City Lib.)

Bill Davis and Katoomba's first ambulance, a 1926 Dodge, which saw earlier service in the Lithgow district. (Mrs V. Davis/Blue Mts. City Lib.)

Ambulance Service

The Katoomba District Ambulance Service began in 1926 when Bill Davis and his wife came from Lithgow. For many years Davis operated with only the one vehicle, a 1926 four-cylinder Dodge, and became skilled in driving at speed over rough mountain roads with potholes "big enough to bury the ambulance". The parameters of the local ambulance officer's duties were very broad indeed in the early years and he was expected to respond with equal speed to broken ankles, injured animals and road accidents.

Bushwalking & the Conservation Movement

During the years of the Great Depression the popularity of walking in the Blue Mountains revived. The impact of the motor car had deflected interest away from the old walking tracks with the general decline in prosperity occurring throughout the community, hiking guides were published alongside road guides and visitors to the Blue Mountains began to rediscover the bush. With the increasing popularity of walking, the early 1930s also saw the emergence of the modern Conservation Movement.

Myles Dunphy, who began walking in the Blue Mountains before World War I, had been influential in forming the Mountains Trails Club in 1914. The members of this club, and the Sydney Bushwalkers Club founded in 1927, had a different view of walking to 'tourist' walkers: the family groups, who strolled the finely crafted tracks close to the centres of settlement.

Dunphy and the Mountain Trailers marked the beginning of a new era of walking in the Blue Mountains. Their emphasis, while still recreational, was on developing the skills of bushcraft, self-reliance and adventure. Earlier walkers who yearned for such elements as part of their walking experience would tramp the Six-Foot Track, the bridle path opened in 1884 to link Katoomba and Jenolan Caves. The new generation of walkers, the 'bushwalkers', left the well-marked tracks and headed into the rougher country, often charting new routes for their comrades to follow.

Public concern for the preservation of the natural environment was sown among the bushwalkers. On the Certificate of Membership of the Mountain Trails Club the following words appeared: "remember, a good bushman is a fellow you will surely want to trail with again. You were not the first over the trail; leave the pleasant places along the way just as pleasant for those who follow you." During the early 1920s, far-sighted Myles Dunphy formulated a plan for a

1930s bushwalkers in Blue Gum Forest which became the subject of a conservation campaign in 1931 and was notified as a public recreation reserve on 2 September, 1932. (A.B. Porter/Blue Mts City Lib.)

Blue Mountains National Park which was adopted by both the Mountain Trails Club, in 1922, and the Sydney Bushwalkers, in 1927.

The Blue Gum Forest, a magnificent stand of tall blue gums growing in the Grose Valley near the junction of Govett's Leap Creek and the Grose River became the subject of what many consider the seminal conservation campaign in 1931 conducted by those whose environmental concern was nurtured in the bushwalking and wildlife societies of the time. It generated considerable interest and co-operation pointing the way for successful future action.

The story of the campaign begins with a chance meeting which occurred during the Easter holidays

of 1931, when a group of bushwalkers led by Alan Rigby entered the forest of blue gums and encountered two men prepared to ringbark the trees. One of the men explained that he had leased the area and planned to replace the blue gums with walnut trees. The walkers were appalled. Those beautiful gums, at the site of Eccleston Du Faur's 1875 Junction Camp, circled by soaring sandstone cliffs, were to be destroyed. Surely the authorities had made a mistake in granting a lease for this purpose. It was a situation that required some fast thinking so, boiling the billy, the walkers discussed the matter over lunch.

It was proposed to seek time to place the issue before the full membership of their bushwalking clubs. There must have been persuasive talkers in the group for the lessee, assured that it would be to his profit, agreed to postpone the ringbarking for the time being. Returning to Sydney, Alan Rigby got things moving with a full report to the next meeting of the Mountain Trails Club. The upshot of this was a request to the Sydney Bushwalkers to assist in a campaign to save the Forest by buying out the lease and ensuring the area be reserved for public use.

When the sanction of the Lands Department was obtained the first step was successfully accomplished. The most difficult task still remained, to raise the one hundred and fifty pounds required by the lessee, C. A. Hungerford of Bilpin, to allow him to obtain an alternative site for his walnut trees. Their agreement called for fifty pounds to be paid by November, 1931, with the balance spread over the following twelve months.

A Blue Gum Committee was established to co-ordinate the campaign. Donations were solicited and fund-raising dances and socials were organised. In a time of economic depression, meeting the lessee's terms proved a difficult job. On Sunday 15 November, a meeting of the committee and Mr Hungerford took place to assess the matter. It was held at the site, among the mighty blue gums whose future was in the balance. Myles Dunphy, a member of the co-ordinating committee, has written about this important gathering. "The business meeting, about midday, was held in pouring rain; the members of the party sat around in a circle in a space between the trees, each shrouded in a cape. The weather was unkind, but the great trees standing up all around appeared magnificent — except one fine specimen which lay stretched out close to the river bank, a victim of the lessee's salesmanship. No doubt it was felled to give point to the necessity for saving the trees."

The meeting resulted in new terms being settled which required payment of a reduced total of one hundred and thirty pounds by the end of December. The committee channelled its energy into a renewed effort and a donation from the Wildlife Preservation Society allowed an immediate deposit to be made.

With the assistance of an anonymous loan to supplement the amount already raised, the deadline was met.

The united action of the bushwalking societies and numerous other supporters had secured a beautiful piece of bushland for public use. The Blue Gum Forest was notified as a public recreation reserve on 2 September, 1932, and a management trust appointed. In 1961, the area was absorbed into the Blue Mountains National Park.

In 1931, the same year that the Blue Gum Forest campaign was being waged, Myles Dunphy formed the National Parks and Primitive Areas Council (NPPAC). Adopting the slogan 'Progress With Conservation', and made up of representatives of all the major bushwalking clubs of the time, the Council set about promoting Dunphy's plan for a Blue Mountains National Park. In August, 1934, it published a four page supplement to the *Katoomba Daily* in which the idea was presented in detail and Dunphy's beautifully drawn map of the proposal was reproduced. Six thousand of these supplements were distributed throughout the Blue Mountains and Sydney.

It still took more than two decades before the plan achieved any kind of reality. The Blue Mountains National Park, comprising much of the central part of the original plan, was gazetted in September, 1959. Over the next twenty years, as a result of intense campaigning on the part of conservationists, further large areas of the Blue Mountains region, including Kanangra-Boyd in the south and Wollemi in the north, were dedicated as national park. By the end of the 1970s, vindicating the vision of the early bushwalker-conservationists, most of the areas covered by the NPPAC proposal had been secured for public recreation.

Boy Scouts, whose movement was inaugurated by Baden-Powell in 1908, improvise a billy holder in the Megalong valley while bivouacking in the 1920s. (H. Colton, Blue Mts Hist. Soc.)

Jenolan Caves

In the mid-1860s the N.S.W. Government, showing considerable vision, announced the creation of a reserve to protect the limestone cave system known then as the Binda or Fish River Caves (Jenolan was not adopted until 1884). This gave official recognition to a part of our country's natural heritage soon to become famous throughout the world.

In the late nineteenth century this isolated spot, tucked away in the wilderness of the south-west Blue Mountains, became one of N.S.W.'s and Australia's great attractions. For overseas and local visitors, a

"On the night of 8th August, Guide Edwards and myself succeeded in getting up the river in the new cave. We built a sort of punt, with four oil drums and some timber, and went up the stream or pool." J.C. Wiburd. (Photographer Charles Kerry/Blue Mts City Lib.)

Above: James Carvosso Wiburd (standing) became Caretaker at the Caves in 1903 and brought with him a thoughtful and analytical approach to the discovery of new caves. When he retired in 1932, this studious, slightly-built man had become something of a legend. With his 'team' of Jack Edwards (seated) and Robert Bailey, his record of discoveries included some of the jewels of Jenolan.

In 1903 he explored the mysterious subterranean River Styx, in what photographer Charles Kerry later referred to as "a small coffin-like box", and discovered the Skeleton Cave with its evidence of an earlier Aboriginal presence at Jenolan. In 1904 he achieved a rare quinella when they uncovered the wonders of The Temple of Baal and The Orient Cave which, in Wiburd's own words, was "the most beautiful cave I have ever seen." The wide-spread opinion that "if Wiburd did not find it, it is not there." (Blue Mts City Lib.)

Below: Jeremiah Wilson, Caretaker at the Caves from 1867 to 1896, was a man who delighted in entertaining his guests. One of his favourite 'tricks' was to decorate the regulation overalls loaned to visitors, with broad arrows and numbers. He was also a caver of great ability, described by visiting journalist Samuel Cook, as a man who "burrowed about like a rabbit" and "wormed his way into the darkness through narrow drives and descended black holes of unknown depths by means of ropes and ladders." (Jim Smith.)

trip to the Caves was an exciting adventure and provided the raw material for numerous newspaper articles, private letters, and journals.

The Fish River/Jenolan Caves were as popular in these early years as Uluru or the Barrier Reef are today. The name was connected with romance. Oliphant Smeaton, a late nineteenth century writer of adventure stories with Australian associations published a novel called *The Treasure Cave of the Blue Mountains*. It is a tale of daring, of young adventurers who find a lost city, gold and jewels in caves beneath the Blue Mountains. The model is clearly Jenolan.

The beginnings of the real story of Jenolan are difficult to discern through a cover of legend and folklore. Oral tradition has it that a bushranger named James McEwan roamed the Oberon-Tarana district in the 1830s stealing from farmers and travellers and then withdrawing to his hideout at Jenolan. When the local settlers, led by the Whalan family, tired of his depredations and organised themselves to track him down, they found him comfortably settled, farming land in a hidden valley.

The story of James McEwan, his arrest and the consequent discovery of the Caves, is well-established in local folklore, though there appears to be no mention of the bushranger in the official records of the time. While McEwan remains a shadowy, though romantic, figure the Whalan's place in the early days of Cave exploration is certain.

From the late 1830s, the Whalans and other families from the Oberon district made exploratory visits to the Caves. While much of their investigation was restricted to the grand natural arches of the daylight caves, they did make some important excursions into the darker regions beyond. With candles and great courage, some of these early explorers ventured into the absolute darkness of the Elder (1848) and Lucas (1860) Caves.

Access to the Caves was severely limited and depended on local knowledge. There was no road and the railway had not yet been extended over the Blue Mountains. Most visitors came across country

Tourists of the 80's visiting Jenolan.

N.S.W. Govt. Tourist Bureau
Cooke Photo.

"In all my travels I have scarcely met anything more wonderful than the Fish River Caves; and the time here was spent so pleasantly, and everyone has been so attentive and obliging to us that we shall always have a happy recollection of the few days we spent in this land of wonders." J.C.'s Visitors Book 1894.
(Blue Mts Hist. Soc.)

on horseback via the Whalan's farm 'Glyndwr' and the family played the role of unofficial guides for many years.

When the railway reached Mount Victoria in 1868 and Tarana in 1872 visitors to the Caves were offered a choice of more established routes. The most popular option was to be met at Tarana by Jeremiah Wilson, appointed 'Keeper of the Caves' in 1867, and travel via his Oberon farm. Alternative routes, including a rough buggy track from Mount Victoria (ca. 1868) and a bridle track from Katoomba (1884), were also available but not as popular.

Competition for the Caves' traffic between centres like Tarana and Mount Victoria was always

*A motoring trip to Jenolan, ca. 1910.
(Blue Mts Hist. Soc.)*

Motoring Fashions — Jenolan Caves.

N.S.W. Govt. Tourist Bureau
Cooke Photo.

A party of visitors to the Jenolan Caves, ca. 1893.
(Blue Mts Hist. Soc.)

Party visiting Jenolan about 1893

preferences returned to Mount Victoria as the destination for the first leg of a Caves excursion from Sydney. The Mount Victoria route was vigorously promoted by the hotel and guesthouse owners and by the multitude of coach operators on the Blue Mountains. As rail times to Mount Victoria became faster and a journey to Jenolan from the city in one day became possible, the use of alternative routes diminished.

Left: No. 1 Caves House with extensions.
Construction of Caves House in 1882 where a visitor in January 1884 "found the one apartment, which serves for dining room, parlor and office, besides being used as a sleeping room, full of a noisy departing crowd, finishing a late breakfast, looking for hats, umbrellas and luggage, paying accounts and talking all at once." (Photographed by Robert Hunt Macleay Museum).

Right: Wilson's Caves House was burned down in 1895 and a new limestone building in Queen Anne style replaced it in 1898. The two storey north eastern wing was completed in 1909 and the four storey Elizabethan style (not here) was constructed in 1918. An assemblage of caves staff clearing up debris after the big flood in May 1916. (Blue Mts Hist. Soc.)

intense. In the 1870s visitors who began their carriage trip from either centre were still faced with an uncomfortable walk down the last steep section to the Caves. In 1879 the Tarana-Caves road was completed and for about ten years that town held the edge over Mount Victoria.

In the late 1880s the Blue Mountains hotel keepers successfully lobbied the Government to improve the road from Mount Victoria and extend it to within half a kilometre of the Grand Arch. In 1896 the road was finally taken through the Arch and travellers'

Accommodation at Jenolan Caves

For over twenty years after Jeremiah Wilson was appointed 'Keeper of the Caves' in 1867 (he was caretaker from 1867 to 1896) there was no accommodation at Jenolan. Visitors were obliged to seek shelter for the night in one of the great arch caves. The Grand Arch was the most popular. In 1869, a large dance platform was built in this cavern and 'smoke concerts' developed into a Jenolan tradition, occasionally revived today.

Here is the scene in the Grand Arch one cold and windy night in the late 1870s.

How very comfortable we were on that and other nights! One man looked after the billy on the fire for tea, another put out tin plates and pannikins, while a third grilled the ham and cold fowl ... we got a good screen round the weather side of the fire, which we heaped up high, and then when we had washed up, every man sat with his pipe and glass of hot grog, and we could afford to laugh over the mishaps of the day.

The regulations of sleeping on these occasions is to lie round the fire heads out, feet in, like the spokes in a wheel, we could not do so, however, the draught was too great ... so still keeping inside the cave we mounted up the rocks to a little nook, where some hay had been laid down, and we slept as best we could, merely removing collars and boots.

The popularity of the Caves demanded the provision of more formal facilities. In 1880 Jeremiah Wilson constructed a sizeable single-storeyed accommodation house of wood and corrugated iron that was divided into a large dining room and five bedrooms. The building could cope with twenty people comfortably while the regular overflow in peak periods slept on the dining room floor, erected tents outside or returned to the time-honoured tradition of camping in the Grand Arch or Devil's Coach House.

As the fame of the Caves spread, additions had to be made to satisfy the standards of the increasing flow of world travellers. In 1887, Wilson constructed a second building, a wooden two-storeyed house capable of handling about thirty more guests.

By the end of the 1880s Jeremiah Wilson presided over a compact little settlement enclosed by mountains and imbued with the romance of wilderness. Visitors could sit on the verandah and listen to the mountain stream racing through a green profusion of ferns next to the house. They could enjoy the well kept gardens planted with exotic trees and shrubs or they could glance upward and contemplate the seemingly perpendicular route by which they had

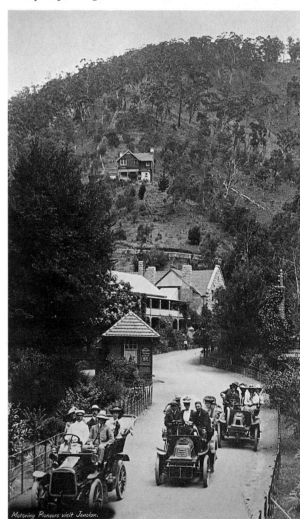

BELOW LEFT: Tourists travelled from the Ivanhoe Hotel at Blackheath, in the newest, up-to-date motor cars, to Jenolan Caves. (Blue Mts Hist. Soc.)

BELOW: Returning to a mountain hotel after a day exploring the caves. (Blue Mts Hist. Soc.)

"Our guide had a lantern with magnesium light, which he constantly cast into dark corners, and through gaping chasms, bringing all sorts of wonderful transparent formations to light." The Duchess of Buckingham & Chandos who visited the Caves in January, 1893. (Blue Mts City Lib.)

descended. They could also buy "all sorts of little necessaries" at a small shop, visit the photographer's studio and even join a circulating library.

In 1894 a total of 1038 visitors signed the Visitors' Book at Caves House. By far the largest number came from New South Wales (572) and the other Australian states (215), while 50 arrived from New Zealand and 164 from Britain. Other countries represented included France, Germany, Africa, America, India, China, Samoa and Fiji.

Among the comments recorded that year were the following:

"Grand sights! Grand guide! Grand everything!"

"Every cave is a palace or a gem; every stream is musical, and the scenery is poetry materialised." (*Mountaineer*, 8 March, 1895.)

In 1895 a fire destroyed Wilson's original accommodation house. A new building of limestone was competed in 1898 after Jeremiah Wilson's term as caretaker had concluded. This now forms the central section of the present Caves House. By 1907 the great interest generated by the discoveries of J. C. Wiburd (caretaker 1903-1932), the opening of new caves like the Temple of Baal and the Orient, and the increasing popularity of the motor car were putting enormous pressure on accommodation facilities. Consequently, Wilson's wooden two-storeyed building was replaced with the present North Wing opened in 1909. Construction of the four-storeyed block that completed the modern complex of Caves House, accommodating over 130 guests, was commenced in 1914 and finished four years later.

Every tourist car stopped at the Hartley Courthouse for the obligatory group photo.
(Blue Mts Hist. Soc.)

Katoomba serviced the Jenolan Caves tourist trade with modern motor vehicles which very quickly supplanted the more leisurely horse-drawn coaches. (Blue Mts Hist. Soc.)

Children rescuing the pumpkins from a flooded vegetable patch. (John Falloon/Blue Mts City Lib.)

Ganbenang Pioneers

The region known as Ganbenang borders the valleys of Hartley and Kanimbla. The Jenolan Caves Road, passing though Lowther and Hampton, runs along its western boundary while the Ganbenang Creek flows into the Cox's River to the east.

In the early days the area was known as Marsden's Swamp, being part of a Crown Grant to the Rev. Samuel Marsden. He made no use of his land and eventually sold it. The early settlers who acquired holdings have engaged in agriculture, cultivating the creek flats and producing mainly maize and potatoes.

In a talk to the Blue Mountains Historical Society in 1949 H.C. Dalziell, a descendent of one of the early landholders, claimed that the name Ganbenang derived from the Gang-Gang parrots which inhabited the area in large numbers in the early years.

He also noted that, for the pioneer women of these outlying districts, "the rearing of their families under the most primitive conditions was a problem they cheerfully undertook." Education, for example, "generally fell to the lot of the mothers" until a school was established at Ganbenang in the 1880s.

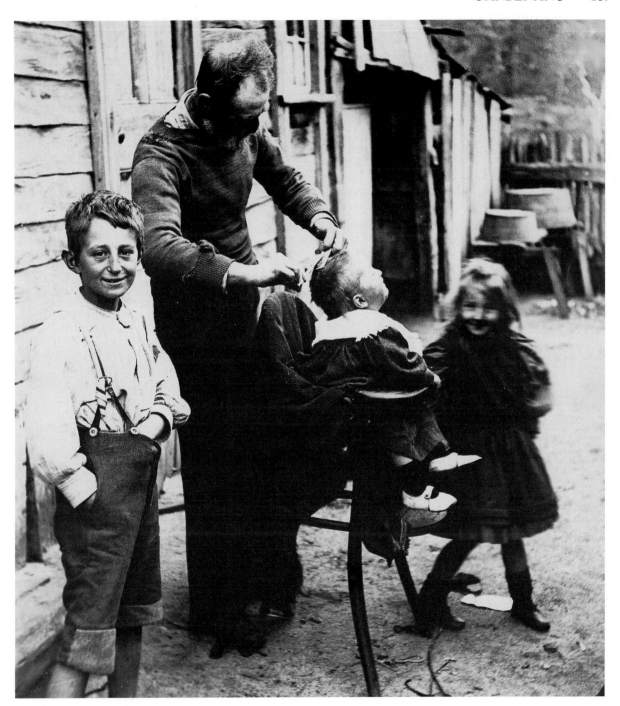

Baby gets a haircut, to the amusement of his brother and sister. (John Falloon/Blue Mts City Lib.)

Private Schools — "Habits of Courtesy & Refinement"

Springwood Ladies College and Osborne Ladies College at Blackheath were two of the private-venture schools and colleges which operated on the Blue Mountains during the period from the late nineteenth century through to the middle of the twentieth.

These non-sectarian schools reflect a colourful, sometimes eccentric, strand in the development of Australian education and their memory is rapidly fading. Most were gone or taken over by church authorities by the 1950s as the dominance of state and religious educational facilities reduced demand for their services. The details of their operations and philosophies survive principally in the memories of former students and documentation is sparse.

Springwood Ladies College was established in 1897 in Moorecourt, the former country residence of Sydney merchant and politician Charles Moore. The longest serving proprietor and headmistress was Mademoiselle Mignon Durand who transferred her Ladies Grammar School in Newcastle to Springwood in the early 1920s. It was she who stamped her personality on the college in no uncertain terms and, by the time the school closed in the 1940s, her name had become almost synonymous with that of the school itself.

"How shall I remember her?" says Joan Glover, a pupil in the secondary school during the 1930s. A short, dark-haired woman of quite "unremarkable appearance, except she knew how to dress She was stylish to my eye and slightly elaborate. There was a certain feeling of theatre a certain merriment about her at times". She always "kept herself very much the headmistress, always kept that distance ... from parents as well as from pupils." Praise was not handed out lightly.

Mile Durand was aiming to produce "women of grace", to "finish" girls in the European manner. "No pains are spared", assured the College prospectus,

Pupils participating in eurhythmic dances in the lovely grounds of Osborne Ladies College.
(Blue Mts City Lib.)

"to train the girls in habits of courtesy and refinement, and to maintain a right moral tone throughout the school." Etiquette, elocution, music and dancing were important subjects. "The music room was very beautiful", Joan Glover remembers. It featured mademoiselle's own baby grand, "draped with a shawl in the mode of the day." Senior students often entertained Mademoiselle's guests with piano and song recitals and girls from Springwood did well at the annual eisteddfods.

After we went back to our families, reflected Joan Glover, life at the school seemed "like a little time slot that didn't happen. I didn't find 'Picnic At Hanging Rock' at all strange!"

Violet Gibbons, head of Osborne Ladies College in Blackheath was also a lady of strong and independent will, remembered as a small, wiry woman with short hair, military bearing and an inclination towards severity. Josie Neville, who as an eight-year-old spent time at Osborne in the mid-

A Junior class of little "Middies" at Osborne Ladies College. (Blue Mts City Lib.)

1930s, recollected that her first impression of Miss Gibbons was of a stern woman "with a frightening glint in her eye."

Osborne College moved from the Sydney suburb of Epping to the Blue Mountains in 1923, establishing itself in a large building that had been constructed in 1888 as the Centennial Hotel. The property possessed expansive views over the Kanimbla and Megalong Valleys and close access to a number of popular bushwalking tracks. The college prospectus proclaimed the virtues of its setting "amidst scenery unequalled in the world over, and in a climate which defies disease." Its location was known to Blackheathens as Paradise Hill.

The cultivation of refined, public spirited young ladies was the goal Violet Gibbons set her school. To achieve this she drew upon her own patriotic passion for Britain and her enthusiasm for the British Navy which became, in the words of a former student, her "magnificent obsession". Not only did her school take its name from the Royal Naval College on the Isle of Wight, but naval jargon, procedure and tradition permeated all aspects of school life.

The girls' dormitories were called "ships" and given the names of such British naval vessels as H.M.S. *Sirius*, H.M.S. *Sydney*, H.M.S. *Revenge* and so on.

A quiet hour in the library of Osborne Ladies College with the Masters of Prose and Poetry. (Blue Mts City Lib.)

The headmistress' own bedroom was H.M.S. *Pelican,* the main assembly room was known as H.M.S. *Nelson* and even the bathroom sailed the seven seas of Miss Gibbon's imagination as H.M.S. *Neptune.* Further, the school's system of authority paralleled a naval structure of command — the younger pupils began as midshipmen, or "middies", the senior students could attain the rank of lieutenant or captain, teachers were the commanders, and Miss Gibbons herself was the Admiral who addressed the assembled crew from the "quarter deck" or the "bridge".

The daily routine at both colleges was characterised by order and Spartan comfort. Zoe Kemmis, a pupil in the junior school at Springwood Ladies College from 1928 to 1930, provides a lively insight into student lifestyles:

At 6 a.m. one girl had the job of ringing the bell. It was 6 o'clock in the summer and 6.30 in the winter. At 6 o'clock we got up and went upstairs to our rooms. I used to sleep on the verandah with five or six other girls downstairs. There were beds all along each side of the verandah, and you went upstairs and there was a washstand in your bedroom with a jug of water. In winter you had a jug or can of hot water and you had to share that and be careful that you didn't take too much One of the senior girls had the job of going down to the copper room and filling up the cans and carrying them all the way up the back stairs and along the verandah and leaving one at each bedroom. At 6.30 another bell went and you had to be washed and dressed by then. At 6.30 you had to do your room, make your bed.

At 7 o'clock if you learnt a musical instrument you might have a half hour practice or you went to half an hour of tennis or you studied. When a bell went for 7.30 you went to study and, if you were always in strife like I always seemed to be, you had to go and sit outside Mademoiselle's bedroom and study so she could tell you weren't talking, somewhere where she could keep an eye on you.

At 8 o'clock a bell went for breakfast where you spoke French only and you said grace before and

The Glen, one of the lovely spots near Osborne Ladies College. (Blue Mts City Lib.)

after meals in French. If you spoke English at any time during the meal you left the room and you didn't have any more breakfast. There was one girl who was a great friend of mine who regularly spoke English in the middle of the meal so we all used to take her pieces of toast and things if we could hide them up our jumpers or somewhere so she'd have something to eat.

After the evening meal, which was only a light meal, we had half an hour of study and half an hour of one of the teachers reading to us. Then we were all taken across to the 'over yonder' (the toilet) by a teacher with a torch and then we went off to bed. If you talked at all after light-out you usually ended up being put in Coventry. You wore a sign around your neck saying 'I am in Coventry. Please do not speak to me'.

At Blackheath the headmistress was a strict disciplinarian whose "lieutenants" patrolled the corridors reporting breaches of regulations and whose morning parades ensured, according to the college prospectus, "that the general appearance of the pupils is up to the standard of the R.N. in cleanliness and smartness." "Polish", recalled Josie Neville, "is the operative word. We polished everything. We polished our shoes, our buttons and our gumboots. Lots of spit and polish."

Marching was a part of the Osborne ritual and, while the girls generally enjoyed banging drums and singing military songs, there were times when such amusement wore thin. Daily exercise was compulsory and the pre-breakfast warm-up often the hardest to take. "It didn't matter how cold it was or whether it was snowing", said Josie Neville, "we all went under the house where we kept our gumboots — cold, cold gumboots — put on raincoats and marched up and down the drive in all kinds of weather and then came back, put our gumboots back on their ledges and our raincoats back on their hooks, and had porridge."

The "Osborne watchers of Blackheath", the locals, have their own memories of this unusual school that existed in their midst for something like thirty years. Nan Smith remembers how the Osborne

girls would arrive at her house to pick laurel leaves, for Miss Gibbons to make into beautiful wreathes for patriotic occasions like Anzac Day or the anniversaries of famous naval battles such as Trafalgar. "The girls used to come along in their very spick and span uniforms and they's ring the front doorbell, and sometimes I'd answer the door and they'd say, almost in unison, 'Good afternoon, Miss Gibbons has asked if we may pick laurel leaves'."

"In a way", concludes Josie Neville, "the marching, the laurel wreaths, the silver buttons, the music, the bands playing and all that — I don't think we were conscious of it being ridiculous. I think children quite like that. I don't think we saw that as particularly different. I think we thought we had the nicest uniforms."

Stratford School, Lawson

In the late 1870s Joseph Hay, a civil servant, acquired 120 hectares of land at Lawson. His residence, built in 1879, provided him with an expansive view across his domain which extended as far as present day Bullaburra. He named his estate 'San Jose'. By 1882 'San Jose' had become 'The Blue Mountains Sanatorium'. In the 1890s it became 'The Palace' guesthouse and was advertised as "absolutely the coolest house on the mountains in summer". In 1919 the 'Stratford Girls School' moved from their small rented cottage into 'The Palace'. The building bore the school's celebrated Shakespearian name proudly on its Castle-like tower, becoming in 1928 an Anglican Grammar School under the management of a Church Council. It continued successfully, with a curriculum spanning the years from Kindergarten to Leaving Certificate, until the mid-1960s. The Anglican Church closed the school and sold the property in 1966. A reception centre and a small community school made subsequent brief appearances in the building, though it was a private residence again by the time fire gutted it on 4 June, 1980. Its ruin can still be seen to the north of Lawson Railway Station. (Opposite: Dr King/Blue Mts City Lib.)

Woodford Academy, Woodford

Few buildings left in the Blue Mountains date before the advent of the railway. When the road provided the only means of travel, the words like 'wild' and 'inhospitable' dominated the accounts of travellers. The Woodford Academy provides a link with this period. The sturdy bulk of its original section has squatted on the Great Western Highway since the early 1840s. It began life as an inn and opened operations under the name of the King's Arms Hotel.

William Buss, the last landlord of the King's Arms was a genial identity in his bright red waistcoat. He would hurry out to welcome an in-coming coach.

After Buss's death in 1867 his family sold the hotel to Alfred Fairfax, a Sydney businessman, who converted the building into a private residence, adding thirty six hectares to the surrounding grounds. Fairfax called his property 'Woodford House', a name which clung to the vicinity.

Fairfax relinquished his property in 1884 and for the next thirty years 'Woodford House' reverted to a boarding house boasting a natural swimming hole, tennis courts and even a golf links. In the 1880s it was advertised as "one of the most complete Establishments on the Mountains".

In 1907, the old building which had lingered for more than sixty years became the 'Woodford Academy' for boys, under the headmastership of educationalist and scholar John McManamey. His special interest was the classics, for which he had won the University Medal, but the school became noted for its commercial subjects.

The chatter and laughter of schoolboys echoed through the halls of the Academy for thirty years until, in the mid-1930s, the school closed and the premises became the private home of the McManamey family. To ensure its future survival, McManamey's daughter vested the property in the National Trust in 1979.

Mt King George.   Mt Hay   Mt Bell   Mt Tomah

View of Public Park from San José

Hay's Cascade Upper Fall

Lawn in front of Sanatorium

Santa Cruz Cottage

Stanley Fall

Hay's Cascade Lower Fall

St Michaels Fall

Sebastian Fall

Cecilia Fall

The Sanatorium

SAN JOSÉ
The Blue Mountain Sanatorium
2400 feet above the Sea 58 Miles only from Sydney
150 Yds from LAWSON Railway Station
The Largest Private Boarding Establishment on The Blue Mountains
The Climate is Cool in Summer and Mild and Invigorating in Winter
and is specially recommended by the Medical Faculty for delicate Constitutions
BATHS, PIANO, SYDNEY DAILY PAPERS, SWINGS, &c.
TERMS,— Most Moderate —— Highest recommendations
Furnished Cottages also Apartments without board if required.

Livingstone Fall

Christabel Fall

Katoomba Public School

The first public school in Katoomba was conducted in a tent for a few weeks in 1882 until bad weather forced removal to a cottage pending the erection of a school building in Parke Street. In 1919 the school became a District School and an Intermediate High School in 1920. Secondary students who previously had to travel to Parramatta, leaving home at 6 a.m. and returning at 8 p.m., were now able to study for their Intermediate Certificate in Katoomba. From 1922 the school also began teaching at senior secondary level up to the Leaving Certificate. The secondary section did not receive full High School status until 1943. Infants, Primary and Secondary departments were all housed in the one school in Parke Street until Katoomba High School moved to its present Martin Street site in 1961. Katoomba Primary School left the old Parke Street buildings for Merriwa Street in the early 1980s.

Woodford Academy in the 1940s.
(Blue Mts Hist. Soc.)

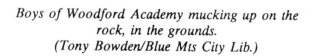

Boys of Woodford Academy mucking up on the rock, in the grounds.
(Tony Bowden/Blue Mts City Lib.)

Above: Secondary students in the unheated classrooms of Katoomba Public School. (Blue Mts Hist. Soc.)

Above right: A shy circle of infants at Katoomba's Superior Public School, ca. 1913. (Harry Phillips/Blue Mts Hist. Soc.)

Springwood's First School

Springwood's first school was opened in 1878 when the town's permanent population was made up mainly of railway workers and farmers. By the end of that year it had an enrolment of fifty four and an average attendance of thirty six. By 1954, when the school moved from its Macquarie Road site to the other end of Springwood and larger premises in Burns Road, the number of students exceeded four hundred. In the photograph right, which dates from 1910 the school pupils are exercising with dumb-bells, a practice possibly introduced by Alfred Matthews, headmaster 1910-1912, whose previous position was on the *Sobraon,* the old sailing ship in Sydney harbour used as a detention centre for wayward boys.

(*Blue Mts City Lib.*)

*Miss Carlon with her pupils at Megalong
Public School, ca. 1910.
(Keith Duncan/Blue Mts City Lib.)*

*The Rowsell family visiting the Megalong
Public School in 1936.
(Marion Brodrick, Blue Mts City Lib.)*

A Right Royal Welcome

In 1934 the Duke of Gloucester visited Australia to participate in Victoria's Centenary Celebrations. During his stay he toured all the Australian states, receiving enthusiastic expressions of loyalty wherever he went. When, on Tuesday 27 November, 1934, the Royal train paused for twenty minutes (ten minutes more than its schedule allowed) at Katoomba, the citizens of the Mountain capital turned on a welcome which, in the opinion of the

Right & below:
Excited children and one naughty boy cheer for the Duke and Duchess of Gloucester and the British Empire as he is greeted at Katoomba Station by the Mayor on November 27, 1934. (Blue Mts Hist. Soc.)

Royal train's Inspector, "exceeded in enthusiasm, and in numbers, that of any other town included in the Royal itinerary."

The Katoomba Daily reported:

One of the largest crowds ever assembled for any function in Katoomba, had taken up position long before the Royal train was timed to arrive — some thousands of school children being given the position nearest to the platform. It was a very gay crowd, with pulses beating fast in anticipation of catching a glimpse of the Royal visitor. Hundreds of flags, bunting to brighten the drab railway surroundings, the bright decorations of the returned soldiers and nurses, the smartly uniformed Scouts and Girl Guides, with banners proudly held aloft, united to form an atmosphere of brightness and cordiality which could not have been excelled.

The Duke smiled at everyone and, walking the full length of the railway platform, won the affection of the crowd "with his unassuming charm and geniality." He signed the autograph book of a young lady whose father had been killed in action during World War I and concluded his visit by declaring

an extra holiday for all the school children who had assembled to welcome him.

The Mayor of Katoomba, Alderman Freelander, gave the Address of Welcome and expressed the "unswerving loyalty and devotion" of his town. "It gives our citizens very great pleasure to welcome you and we know that they will long cherish the recollection of this day."

When the Royal train pulled out the Duke took with him a specially inscribed album of Harry Phillips's photographs to remind him of his brief stop in the Blue Mountains.

Right: "... and then the arrival of the Royal Progress ... the sight of the white gloved hand in the distance and my complete disregard for anything else until I saw Her Majesty for the first time ... I had a lump in my throat and my eyes were misty ... I had seen the Queen of Australia for a few fleeting seconds ..." Blue Mountains Advertiser, *18 February, 1954. (Blue Mts City Lib.)*

Left: When the Royal train steamed into Lawson in August, 1920, H.R.H. Edward Prince of Wales was on the engine having driven it part of the way from valley Heights. The Blue Mountains Echo *of 13 August, 1920, reported, "The Prince, catching sight of an old man in full khaki regimentals and wearing on his breast a row of medals, barely waited until the engine stopped before he jumped to the ground and approached Duncan Allen. Moreover, His Royal Highness wiped his hands in a most democratic fashion on a lump of cotton waste and, finally, completed the task by rubbing them on his riding trousers. That done, he shook Duncan warmly by the hand." (Blue Mts Hist. Soc.)*

Horticulture in the Blue Mountains

The Blue Mountains, as we know them today, were formed over millions of years, undergoing drastic changes in many different periods. Once the area was a series of low lying lakes and swamps with a thick build-up of silts; these gradually dried, compressing the silt into solid sandstone with shale and coal deposits.

Then great pressures caused gigantic uplifts, slowly pushing the entire area upwards in a monoclinal fold to heights of a 1000 metres. However, the land was flatter, with undulating contours. Rivers formed leaving further deposits of sand. Then, as the rivers gradually cut their way into the area, erosion by wind and extreme heat and cold did the rest, forming the vast gorges and sheer cliff walls which are the grandeur of the Blue Mountains today.

Isolated volcanic eruptions also took place leaving rich deposits of basalt in areas such as Mt Wilson, Mt Tomah, Mt Banks and others, creating a richer, more fertile growth of vegetation than on the sandstone ridges. Except for these isolated basalt areas, and sheltered valleys and gullies where the soil deposits are richer, the sandstone plateaus of the mountains are generally poor in soil nutrients, supporting dry sclerophyll and heath vegetation.

It is no wonder then that the early white settlers made little attempt to farm in the mountains, using them mainly as a route from Sydney to the pastoral areas of the west, such as Bathurst and Orange. No doubt some planting of fruit trees and growing of vegetables took place in these early times, but never enough to support the local population. The only exception to this was the period of Chinese market gardens between 1890 and 1930.

With the building of the railway over the mountains in the 1860s easier access was made possible and the mining of coal in the 1870s helped to expand the population. It was not until the 1880s, with the coming of wealthy and influential people

'Lilianfels' orchard, ca. 1915, during the Kemp ownership. The fomally layed out and carefully tendered orchard existed up until the subdivision of this property in 1921. The clipped laurel hedge with archway still exists. Remnants of this orchard, some large hazelnut bushes and a huge Spanish chestnut tree may still be seen in the Lilianfels Park. (Mr Andrew Kemp)

from Sydney that horticulture gained momentum. Well-to-do merchants and officials began to build permanent and holiday houses; many were anxious to impress, not only with lavish housing, but with gardens worthy of admiration. They spent vast amounts of money and time clearing the land to establish orchards and gardens based on traditional English styles, with imported exotic trees and plants. They paid little or no attention to harmonising with the indigenous flora.

The Anglo-European style of gardening was to continue and dominate up to the present day, with spasmodic attempts to retain the natural vegetation. However, a conscious effort to preserve the natural areas in the mountains has gradually taken hold, culminating in preservation having become a contentious and political issue today. In the early days the die was cast and many large gardens were established; some survive today, wholly or in part: at 'Yester Grange' in Wentworth Falls, at 'Lilianfels' in Katoomba, at 'Nooroo' and 'Yengo' and in many other fine gardens at Mt Wilson.

An interesting article in the *Illustrated Sydney News*, dated February 20th, 1890, shows the temper of the times:

> Mr S.H. Hyam, corn merchant of Sydney, is another of those who evidently intend to make of Katoomba their future home. He has cleared and cultivated some three acres of land, rich chocolate soil sprinkled as it were with a thin deposit of stones, which at first glance made it look anything but promising, more especially as it was so densely timbered that nothing but straggling tufts of grass were enabled to drag out an existence. His experiments have shown the fallacy of a hasty judgement, for the vegetables, fruit and flowers which have rewarded his efforts testify to the splendid producing qualities of the soil.

The trees and plants grown in these gardens consisted mainly of conifers and deciduous trees such as elms, oaks, beeches, birches and maples, evergreens such as arbutus and laurel. Along with other exotics, these still dominate the modern garden layout. The plants for the gardens were brought from early established nurseries around Sydney. By the 1890s several plant nurseries had been established in the mountains. In 1895 Mr R.M. Pitt was growing and supplying daffodils and lilies for sale from his property 'Coorah' (now the Church of England Grammar School) at Wentworth Falls.

One of the earliest known landscape gardeners in the Blue Mountains was Alexander A. Spahno, born in Costa Rica in 1862. He moved to the mountains in the 1880s establishing nurseries at Wentworth Falls and Lawson, using them as bases for the development and planting of large gardens such as 'Holmwood' at Leura and 'Cherrywood' at Wentworth Falls, 'Rainbow Lodge' (formerly 'Yama') at Hazelbrook, and possibly 'Whispering Pines' at Wentworth Falls and 'Lilianfels' at Katoomba. This early landscaper was remembered by locals up to the early 1930s; his name is all but forgotten today.

Over the ensuing years many plant nurseries were established in various mountain towns, many still operating today: Thew, Turner, Kerslake and Harris

The Blackheath Memorial Park occupies a site that served originally to water stock. When the railway was built in the 1860s the area was reserved as a source of water to supply the steam engines and a dam was built. Eventually the railway abandoned their dam for an alternative supply. The site was subsequently gazetted as a Reserve for recreation in 1919 and eventually drained and landscaped as a 'Memorial' to the Blackheath men who had enlisted in World War I. In 1929 work also began on converting the old railway reservoir into a community swimming pool. The official opening took place at the end of 1931 and the park and pool have since become a popular picnic location, particularly during the Blackheath Rhododendron Festival in November. (Mitchell Lib.)

Blackheath Gardens and School of Arts in 1922, soon after the World War I gun was installed. (Jean Caldwell/Blue Mts City Lib.)

at Blackheath; Bewley, Milton and Gaibor at Wentworth Falls. Gaibor's Nursery at Wentworth Falls was formerly "The Pottery Patch" run by two women, Dorothy Commins and Valerie Murray for nearly twenty years, Meers at Bullaburra, Moffat at Springwood and Newports at Winmalee.

Of all the nurseries established in the mountains, the one started by Paul Sorensen at Leura in the early 1920s was by far the most famous. Sorensen, born in Copenhagen in 1890, trained and worked in many famous gardens in Denmark, came to Australia in 1915, and moved to Katoomba circa 1917 to be the gardener at the Carrington Hotel. Paul Sorensen became a legend, named 'Australia's Master Gardener'. He planned and created many fine gardens not only in the mountains but in other parts of New South Wales, and many of these still flourish today. The masterpiece among his mountain gardens is probably 'Everglades' at Leura, now a National Trust property. Beautiful bookleaf stone retaining walls, winding paths and lawned terraces carved out

Construction of the Garden Theatre, Everglades, early 1930s. (Blue Mts City Lib.)

Hinkler Park

Hinkler Park, named in honour of the Australian aviator Herbert 'Bert' Hinkler (1892-1933), whose solo flight from England to Australia in February 1928 captured the imagination of the nation, was officially opened on Tuesday 27 November, 1934. This was the day the Duke of Gloucester paid his brief visit to Katoomba and the Katoomba Daily reported: "After the departure of the Royal train, a procession was formed of returned soldiers, Scouts, Girl Guides and school children and, headed by the Band, marched down Katoomba and Lurline Streets to the park. A big proportion of the crowd present comprised children, and the new playground equipment underwent a searching test. They appeared to have the time of their lives." A commemorative plaque was unveiled by the aviator's mother, Mrs F. A. Hinkler, who had travelled down from her home in Bundaberg, Queensland. "He loved Katoomba", she said, "and formed the opinion that the scenery both for grandeur and beauty was unsurpassable." Bert Hinkler had died in 1933 when his plane crashed in Italy and all present hoped that the park, named after this Australian hero of the air, "would be an inspiration to thousands of children who would use the playground." *(Blue Mts Hist. Soc.)*

of a hillside with spectacular views of the valley, and natural bush walks leading to a grotto, are among the many fine features of this seven hectare property. After his death in 1983, Sorensen left to the mountains a legacy of garden design, unseen on such a scale before, and probably not to be seen again.

Another aspect of horticulture was the establishment of many fine orchards mainly at Blackheath, Shipley, Hartley and Megalong, many of which still thrive.

After World War I, a rush of civic pride affected local councils and residents, and the creation of municipal parks and gardens went on into the 1950s. The Memorial Park and the Community Hall Gardens at Blackheath, Kingsford Smith, Russell Hawke and Hinkler Parks at Katoomba, Gloria Park at Hazelbrook and Buttenshaw Park at Springwood are among the better known municipal parks dating from this era.

Garden clubs and horticultural societies also sprang up in most of the larger mountains towns; the Blackheath and District Horticultural Society, established in 1920, still operates. The flower shows staged by these societies are not only pleasurable and informative but provide a much-patronised community activity. Garden festivals such as the Blackheath Rhododendron Festival (established 1953) and the Leura Garden Festival, which started in the 1960s, are still held annually. Thousands of people visit the festivals as well as the many fine private gardens open to the public, and mountain horticulture has a national and international reputation.

In more recent years the Bacchante Gardens have been established at Blackheath by the Blue Mountains Rhododendron Society — set in natural bushland, growing mainly rhododendrons, azaleas and allied species. The Mt Tomah Botanic Garden has been opened as a cold climate arboretum annex to the Royal Botanic Gardens in Sydney.

The Blue Mountains has yet to fully realise the potential of horticulture as a relatively non-polluting industry. However careful planning and management are needed to blend both exotic and native vegetation which are equally important to the well-being and survival of this unique area. In broad terms the ideal situation for the Mountains is that of houses among trees, rather than trees among houses.

Colin Slade

Kingsford Smith Park, ca. 1936. A landscape plan was drawn up by Mr Kerr from Sydney Botanic Gardens, labour came from the unemployed and stone to build the many retaining walls was brought by truck from nearby bush areas. It was officially opened by the Hon. L.O. Martin, M.L.A. Minister for Works and Local Government, on 1 January, 1940. By 1947 the park was refurbished with a pond, a music shell and a children's playground. In recent years severe vandalism took place until a committee of local concerned residents formed with the ambition to restore the park. The two-storeyed house in the centre, belonged to Mr Hudson, after whom the original gully was named. (Photographed by A.E. Manning/Mr Ib Sorenson)

The Blue Mountains and the Ashes

When Australia defeated England for the first time in a Test match on English soil in August 1882, the death and cremation of English cricket was announced in the "Sporting Times". It was not until a hastily re-vamped English side visited the colonies during the Australian summer of 1882-1883 that the real 'Ashes' came into existence. The English, captained by Ivo Bligh (later Lord Darnley), restored their country's honour by winning the three-Test series and, before returning home, were presented with three items that now occupy a central place in the folklore of Anglo-Australian cricket: some ashes, supposedly of one of the Third Test bails, a small pottery urn, and an embroidered red velvet bag.

The story of the red velvet bag, in which the urn containing the ashes was placed, is linked with one of the prominent families of early Katoomba. It was the gift of Mrs Ann Fletcher whose husband, John W. Fletcher, was running a school in the Sydney suburb of Woollahra at the time of the Test series. A year later, in 1884, the Fletchers moved to Katoomba where they opened The Katoomba College, a boarding school for boys. It was located in the building that was later to become The Royal Coffee Palace and finally, before its demolition in the early 1960s, the headquarters of the Blue Mountains City Council.

The Fletchers were active in the life and affairs of Katoomba throughout the 1880s, until the depression of the early 1890s forced the school's closure in 1893. The name of the building was then changed to The Priory and Mrs Fletcher ran it as a boarding house until 1896 when the family returned to Sydney. Sport was a strong interest in the Fletcher family. John Fletcher played most games well. He was influential in establishing soccer and golf in Australia. The Fletcher's eldest son, John Williams, played cricket for Paddington with Victor Trumper and later represented Queensland in 1909-1910.

A close friend of the family was Yorkshire-born watercolourist William Blamire Young. It is thought he was the designer of the embroidery pattern that decorates the red velvet bag as he often created designs for Mrs Fletcher. He, was also a resident of Katoomba in the 1880s, being appointed assistant master at Katoomba College in 1885. A letter from Ivo Bligh thanking Mrs Fletcher for her gift is housed with the other relics at Lords.

Bradman at Blackheath

On Monday 2 November, 1931, a special cricket match took place on the oval at Blackheath, between teams representing the local community and Lithgow. Organised by the Blackheath Municipal Council, the event was used to christen the newly installed malthoid wicket, the first of its kind in the Western districts. In the Blackheath team were Test

The Coffee Palace, ca. 1910, once housed the Katoomba College, and the Blue Mountains City Council. (Blue Mts City Lib.)

players Oscar Wendell Bill and Donald Bradman who had been specially invited for the occasion. The photograph shows Don Bradman (arms folded, centre) prior to his cutting the ribbon to open the new pitch. Next to him in the suit is Peter Sutton, Blackheath's Mayor, and on his other side Wendell Bill. Few in the crowd were prepared for the memorable match that followed, memorable simply because of the exploits of 'The Don' who, in his own words, "had a day out". And what a day it was! In one three over period, in which he faced twenty-two balls, The Don hit ten sixes, nine fours, a two and two singles, running up what was probably the fastest century ever scored. He was finally caught on 256, an innings that ensured a Blackheath victory. The bat Bradman used in this match was later given to Mayor Sutton who had it mounted on the wall of the Council offices in Blackheath. A story survives that he occasionally asked people to swear on it when a truthful response was required.

The Blue Mountains District Rugby League Team, 1929

When Katoomba entered a rugby league team successfully in the Hartley District competition in 1915, the 'professional' code in Australia was only seven years old. A strong League tradition emerged in the Blue Mountains and spectators witnessed some intense rivalry between teams representing several of the local communities. Springwood, Leura, Katoomba and Blackheath all fielded teams in a local competition under the control of the Blue Mountains District Rugby League. From various local sides a District team was chosen to represent the Blue Mountains against neighbouring areas and sometimes against some of the Sydney clubs. 'The Blues', as they were known, were generally a strong team and achieved considerable success during the 1920s and 1930s.

One of The Blues' star players for many years was Aboriginal winger Jackie Brooks whose "sparkling play brought down the house again and again". He was speedy, had "a bit of pace in reserve" and was also a capable defender. This "spectacular little winger", as one sports writer summed him up, was a popular identity in Katoomba and worked for many years in the kitchens of the Carrington Hotel.

At the age of eleven he was awarded a medal for his bravery in the rescue of two other boys who had fallen from a cliff on Narrow Neck. His strong singing voice was also admired and he was reputed to be a fine dancer. He left Katoomba in the early 1960s, spending the remainder of his life in Redfern.

Left: Bradman (centre) in Blackheath in 1931.
(Blue Mts City Lib.)

The Katoomba Baths were opened ca.1912 near the Meeting-of-the-Waters between Katoomba and Leura. Now filled in as a park, the area is a popular picnic spot. In the background is the Chelmsford Bridge, one of the first locations to be floodlighted as a night-time tourist attraction, in the 1930s. (Photographer: Harry Phillips/Blue Mts Hist. Soc.)

Writers in the Blue Mountains

Traditional surveys of Blue Mountains writing begin with travellers' accounts of scenery and topography of the area. Earliest descriptions occur in letters, journals and verses of settlers on the Sydney side of the mountains. The poet Barron Field and other contemporaries of Governor Macquarie recounted travels and scenery across to the Bathurst side. The poet James Tompson invoked the Emu Plains scenery; as settlement extended in the mountains, travellers like Charles Darwin and imaginative writers like Charles Harpur drew on the surroundings.

By 1900 the Blue Mountains had been visited, and described in passing, by Darwin, Mark Twain and other international figures. Sir Henry Parkes, N.S.W. Premier, was more typical of writers who maintained establishments in the region before that date, celebrating in verse the natural beauty of favoured locations. The scenic aspects of the Blue Mountains still compel full-time and part-time residents to inscribe conventional sensations. Notable contributors to this tradition have included Katoomba poet Harry Peckman (friend of Henry Lawson), the Blaxland printer-poet B.F. Cummins and Leura versifier Minnie Brackenreg. The poetry of Mark O'Connor and other occasional residents maintains this 'picturesque' and sublime strain.

The 'forbidding' landscape, 'swirling mists' and 'hidden caves' provided a backdrop for adventure stories and romances like Oliphant Smeaton's *The Treasure Cave of the Blue Mountains* published at the turn of the twentieth century, or the thrillers produced by Frank Walford during his long residence at Katoomba. A gothic strain in fiction stems from early transformations of Aboriginal and convict-era sites and the dreams of settlers who imposed Victorian and Edwardian architectural follies on the landscape. The fire-damaged ruins at 'Eurama' at Faulconbridge serve as the site for

Margaret Paice's fine children's novel *Dolan's Roost*. The railway across the Mountains and the development of bushwalking as a recreation also gave rise to celebratory and imaginative works.

Works by resident writers have offered more than emotional snapshots, and have dwelt on the distinctive character of settlers and settlements. Walford's novels examined the lives of town dwellers and drew on local politics, scandals and murders, to present a side of everyday life which was ignored by the 'swirling mist' writers. Margaret Trist, Blaxland resident in the late 1930s and early 1940s, also put the fictive town of Upper Glen under the microscope in *Now That We're Laughing* and a series of short stories inlcuding *A Village Dictator*. Trist described the comic side of village life, as well as the loneliness of wives cut off from social pleasures while their men commuted to the city.

Nancy Phelan's novella *Home is the Sailor* explores the lives of residents of the fictional village

Kylie Tennant lived at Shipley from 1974 until her death in 1988. (Blue Mts City Lib.)

of Hazel Falls, and the remarkable inhabitants of the geriatric hospital, Baskerville Hall. In 1921, the short-story writer Margaret Fane described the Red Cross Hospital, Bodington at Wentworth Falls in quite a different light, inviting readers of her regular columns in the *P.F.A. Quarterly* to contribute to the welfare of the returned soldiers there. Fane also wrote of Rhonda Valley, where she moved in 1921.

Other writers and artists moved to the Mountains in the early decades of the twentieth century to escape city distractions. Norman Lindsay came to Faulconbridge in 1912 to produce the bulk of his life's work, including numerous novels; visitors who came to his house inlcuded the poets Leon Gellert, Hugh McCrae and Douglas Stewart.

At Glenbrook, the short-story writer Hilary Lofting (brother of *Dr Dolittle* author Hugh Lofting) settled in 1917, before moving on to other locations inlcuding Rhonda Valley and Faulconbridge, where he lived with Margaret Fane. Lofting's stories described the arrival of unemployed travellers in the early twenties: one visitor, 'The Piper', had the knack of whistling bird songs so that he was never lonely on the track. Another visitor stayed at Rhonda Valley for three days, doing work about the house.

Lofting also described the Swaggies Cave:

The Swaggies' Cave is a beautiful place — practically a drawing room with running water. It is a pocket in the limestone wall which guards the Bathurst Road between Lawson and Wentworth Falls. Ti-tree hangs over it and stands sparsely before it, and a little mountain spring bubbles and chuckles in one corner of it. In midsummer as in winter the spring is alive, so you are certain of ice-cold filtered water. There is plenty of room for a man to stretch out, with good shelter from the westerlies, a red and yellow roof to keep off the rain, and the ti-tree veil to keep out the sun. There is even a little patch of grass for a lawn in front, with a telegraph pole to lean against while the billy boils. The cave floor is a couple of feet above the level of the road, which makes it safe for passing traffic, and the whisper of the spring is companionable through the night when there is no traffic. A beautiful place.

('Safety', *Bulletin*, 27 April 1922)

Glenbrook developed into something of a writer's and artists' village, with the arrival of poets David McKee Wright and Zora Cross, and painters Mick Paul and Dorothy Ellsmore Paul in the 1920s. Their visitors included Christopher Brennan, Hugh McCrae, Jack Lindsay and John Le Gay Brereton, whose *Landlopers* (1899) and *Knocking Round* (1930) recorded notable walks to the Jenolan Caves and around the Lower Mountains. Other literary residents of the Lower Mountains included Judge A.B. Piddington, *Lone Hand* editor Walter Jago and Alec Chisholm, who were familiars of Wright, Cross and the Trists. Zora Cross planted Queensland shrubs, trees and flowers about the property 'Greeanawn' she shared with Wright and described the effect in numerous of her lyrics. She also described the Blue Pool at Glenbrook:

I came upon a pool as still as air —
A blue lagoon, cool-chaste as moonlit jade.
My footsteps on the brink no echo made,
And there was not one murmur anywhere.
The quiet dusk unbound her soft, brown hair,
A noiseless leaf fell through the cool, green shade;
And one long slender shadow seemed to wade
In soundlessness across the stillness there. ...
'The Blue Lagoon', *Bulletin,* 31 January 1924.

The connections between writers in the Mountains suggest that isolation had diminished through the 1920s and 1930s. Margaret Trist and her husband Frank ('Jack Bush' to readers of his children's tales) were on friendly terms with Eleanor and Eric Dark at 'Varuna' in Katoomba. The Trists met the American poet Karl Shapiro at 'Varuna' during the Second World War, and Shapiro celebrated his friendship with the Darks in poems published in Australian journals. Eleanor Dark's own view of the Blue Mountains is well put in *The Little Company* (1945):

In the mountains, nights were long and dark and piercingly cold; days were rent and maddened by bitter westerly winds. In the early morning taps were frozen, the ground stood up on tiny stilts of ice, and pavements rang like iron underfoot. Down in the gullies where the sun came late or never, plants and

Eleanor Dark with the manuscript of The Timeless Land *outside 'Varuna' which is a writers' centre today. (M. Dark/Blue Mts City Lib.)*

undergrowth were no longer green, but powdery white — brittle and unearthly like frost flowers. Under the towering tree-ferns, among the mossy rocks and decaying logs, the lyrebird, embodiment of a perpetual green twilight, stressed the silence with his midwinter song of mating. The smell was of loamy soil, rich with the rotting leaves of centuries.

Up on the tableland above those wide gullies and narrow gorges the sun shone through an air so icily pure that every breath of it was to the lungs like the shock of cold water to the body; there was a shiver in the thinnest tracery of shade. Shopkeepers strayed to their doorways to loiter for a moment in the sunshine, rubbing their numbed fingers. Postmen and tradesmen were more leisurely on their rounds, housewives dallied when they came out to shake their mats, and holiday makers, stretched deck-chairs on boarding-house verandahs, basked rapturously, newspapers and knitting forgotten on their knees. Afternoons died quickly under lengthening shadows, and sudden sunsets, as gorgeous as mountain parrots, flamed out across the purple valleys. When they faded only a cold, bluish haze was left, and smoke began to rise from every chimney to meet and mix with it. People retreated indoors to huddle over fires, leaving the streets deserted, the town beleaguered by darkness.

The novelist Eric Lowe lived close to the Darks in Cascade Street, Katoomba; the writer Nina Lowe was interviewed in 1930 at 'Varuna' by Zora Cross for her series of pen-portraits of Australian women writers published in the *Australian Woman's Mirror*. Cross's interviews revealed to the general public the sheer number of women writers who were likely to be otherwise relegated to the margins. Ethel Turner was one of her subjects; Turner vacationed in the Upper Mountains with her friend, novelist Louise Mack, before the Great War. Both Turner and Mack used the Blue Moutains as a setting for children's tales. Turner eventually established a holiday retreat at Leura, close to the Evatt's home, 'Leuralla'. As early as 1910, David McKee Wright had celebrated a picnic at Leura with college friends of Zora Cross. Novelists of Margaret Trist's generation, including Eve Langley, Dymphna Cusack, Kylie Tennant and

Greville Texidor, added to the Mountains' renown as a writers' locality. Tennant's collaborations and interests reflect the thematic links and relationships between writers; among her works is the biography of Herbert Vere Evatt.

The Mountains clearly exercised appeal as a work-place for writers long before the arrival of current literary residents like Kit Denton, Nancy Phelan, Kate Llewellyn, Dorothy Porter and Richard Neville. The convenience of a railway connection to Sydney has always recommended the move. The impact on literary production of residence in the Mountains has sometimes been direct, but more often obliquely reflected. Henry Lawson's work at Mount Victoria gave rise to early poems on locality. Thomas Kenneally's 1964 novel *The Place at Whitton* concerned residence at the Springwood Seminary, where Edmund Campion also trained for the priesthood. Gabrielle Lord lived at Glenbrook until her first novel publication. Between the polarities of a place to write about and a place to write in, the Blue Mountains have had a critical impact on Australian culture in general. The influence of the Mountains increased with the establishment of 'Varuna' as a writers' centre at Katoomba in 1989. Among early guests, Gabrielle Lord, Alan Close, Judith Lukin and Yasmine Gooneratne located an environment to advance their projects, so that results of patronage may be reflected in future work.

As well, local history groups, writers' workshops and educational institutions have, in recent years, constituted a strong support and resource, reflecting the region's consciousness of what it materially owes to writers' efforts.

Michael Sharkey

Fiction with Blue Mountains Locations

BASTIAN, Greg, *Lies and Alibis,* Brisbane, U.Q.P., 1992.

BRINSMEAD, Hesba, *Longtime Passing*, Sydney, A&R, 1971.

BRINSMEAD, Hesba, *Longtime Dreaming*, Sydney, A&R, 1982.

BRINSMEAD, Hesba, *Christmas at Longtime,* Sydney, A&R, 1983.

BRINSMEAD, Hesba, *A Saphire for September,* London, O.U.P., 1967.

BURROWS, Denys, *Stagecoach West,* Sydney, The Educational Press, 1964.

BUTLER, Richard, *A Dangerous Summer,* Adelaide, Rigby, 1982.

CUSACK, Dymphna, *Say No To Death*, London, Heinemann, 1951.

CUSACK, Dymphna & JAMES, Florence, *Four Winds and a Family,* Melbourne, Lansdowne, 1965.

DARK, Eleanor, *The Little Company*, Sydney, Collins, 1945.

ELLIOTT, Sumner Locke, *Edens Lost,* London, Michael Joseph, 1970.

FOSTER, David, *The Pure Land,* Melbourne, Macmillan, 1974.

HATHORN, Libby, *Valley Under The Rock,* Melbourne, Heinemann, 1993.

HOWARD, Tom, *The Health Farm Murders,* Sydney, Rastar Press, 1985.

KRAUTH, Nigel, *JF Was Here,* Sydney, Allen & Unwin, 1990.

LAWSON, Henry, *Grandfather's Courtship, A Christmas Story,* Sydney, A&R, 1982.

MASS, Nuri, *Donna Roon*, Sydney, Alpha Books, 1970.

MASS, Nuri, *The Wizard of Jenolan,* Sydney, A&R, 1946.

McCULLOUGH, Colleen, *The Ladies of Missalonghi,* London, Hutchinson, 1987.

PAICE, Margaret, *Dolan's Roost,* Sydney, Collins, 1974.

PHELAN, Nancy, *Home is the Sailor,* Melbourne, Hyland, 1987.

ROWE, Jennifer, *Grim Pickings,* Sydney, Allen & Unwin, 1987.

SMEATON, Oliphant, *The Treasure Cave of the Blue Mountains,* Edinburgh, Oliphant, Anderson & Ferrier, n.d.

TRIST, Margaret, *Now That We're Laughing,* Sydney, A&R, 1945.

TURNER, Ethel, *Laughing Water,* London, Ward Lock, 1920.

TURNER, Ethel, *In the Mist of the Mountains,* London, Ward Lock, 1908.

Norman Lindsay

The Blue Mountains was a place conducive to thought and creativity for Norman Lindsay. In 1911, hoping that the Mountain air would restore his failing health, he arrived with his wife-to-be, Rose Soady. After a short period at Leura the couple moved to Faulconbridge. On one of his regular rides in the bush Lindsay discovered the stone cottage that has now become one of the most visited places on the Blue Mountains.

'Maryville', as the house was then known, was owned by Francis Foy and was in a state of some disrepair. Following its purchase for five hundred pounds in 1912, Lindsay immediately began to impose his own character upon the property. The next fifty years saw numerous changes to the main building and the gradual evolution of the grounds where Lindsay, "dab-dab-dabbing away like a swallow", populated the gardens with statuary, constructed bush pathways and excavated the large swimming pool.

Springwood became the centre of Lindsay's rich creative life. This small, seemingly frail man expended his boundless energy and enthusiasm on a range of artistic media including oils, watercolour, pen and ink, etching, sculpture, ship models, and writing. To use his creative abilities to the full was his purpose in life. He was never idle for he never stopped working; there were simply not enough hours in the day.

At first glance Lindsay's art may seem to have little connection with the Blue Mountains but the landscape clearly provided an environment in which his vision of heroic Man was nurtured. The Blue Mountains was 'sublime', it was grand, it was mysterious and it was dangerous. It invited Man to contemplate his place in the scheme of things. The climate was also conducive to physical fitness and hygienic living, substantial motives for settlement in the region. Mountain air could 're-create' and refresh the mind and body.

In his art Lindsay's own human frailty was submerged in a celebration of human creative spirit. His sculptures of mythic beings and the voluptuous women and muscular pirates and soldiers who populate his pictures, all reveal an essentially pagan delight in the vitality of life and the virtues of physical health.

The Lindsays were renowned for their hospitality and a rich social life also flourished at Springwood with numerous visitors coming and going. The poet Douglas Stewart recalled his own visits to Springwood:

> I think of evenings when he strolled far over the lawns with three or four cats frisking about him, to get eggs or milk from Nosworthy's across the road; and best of all, for I have always loved the sound of water, I remember long afternoons by the fishpond, listening to the splashing of the fountain and talking of whatever was in Lindsay's mind at the time, usually the latest Australian poems, novel and short stories, or sometimes of his friends who had visited him at Springwood long before our days — Gruner, J. F.

Above left: George Finey, assisted by artist Malcolm King, paints his 'Fish' mural on a Springwood bus shelter to mark the centenary of Springwood Railway Station in 1984. (Blue Mts City Lib.)

Above right: Norman Lindsay and his henchman Harry McPhee, who was the curator of The Norman Lindsay Gallery and Museum until 1993. (Harry McPhee/Blue Mts City Lib.)

Archibald, Blamire Young, Raynor Hoff, Kenneth Slessor, Hugh McCrae ...

When Lindsay died at the age of ninety, on 21 November, 1969, he left a substantial selection of his work to the National Trust on the condition that it purchase his property to house the bequest. A public appeal was successful in raising the required sum of money and, on 24 February, 1973, the Norman Lindsay Gallery and Museum was officially opened by the Governor-General Sir Paul Hasluck.

George Finey

George Finey was born in Auckland, New Zealand, in 1895 and, after serving in World War I, came to Australia in 1919. He soon became one of the leading black and white artists of his day, his cartoons and caricatures appearing in numerous papers and magazines including *Smith's Weekly*, *The Bulletin* and *The Labor Daily*. In the mid-1940s Finey and his family moved to the Blue Mountains where his passion for art and his good-humoured larrikinism soon made him a familiar figure. He explored a diversity of artistic media including pen and ink, ceramics, paint and collage, and worked with considerable energy to encourage the creative impulse in children. He died at his home in Lawson in 1987, aged ninety-two years.

The 'Steamed' Fish

In the popular mythology of the Blue Mountains one of the richest sources of anecdote has always been the commuters' special, the legendary 'Fish'. The argument surrounding its name has been a long and enduring one. The most commonly accepted tradition has it that the name derives from an engine driver stationed at Penrith in the mid-1860s. John Heron built himself a reputation for speed on the run between Sydney and the station that was then the terminus of the Western line.

The big Scot's name, so the story goes, underwent a local corruption to 'Herring' and, as his whistle challenged the signals at Penrith, the cry would go up: "Here comes the big fish!" Ultimately the name transferred to the train. When the railway was extended over the Blue Mountains this name stuck

to the morning and evening express services which operated between Mount Victoria and Sydney.

Over the years this particular train became, in the words of Alan Lewis, a Springwood artist and Fish commuter, "like a sort of club on wheels really." In an interview for the Blue Mountains City Library he recalled how: "They used to have a buffet car on and you could get tea and toast for a shilling. Very often that would be people's breakfast. They wouldn't have time to have their breakfast. There was one guy living up near me I remember — he used to come running to the train with his collar and everything in one hand. Several like this would rush in, very often going into the lavatory to shave and finish the rest of their toilet, and then they'd order their tea and toast. When it went up to one and sixpence everyone was horrified."

Compartments became small social clubs and

seats were guarded jealously. "There was great rivalry between all the different parts of the train, you know," commented Alan Lewis. In this reflection he is supported by another Springwood commuter who experienced life on the old 'steamed' Fish, Bede Loneragan. He recalled that any attempt at socialising beyond one's own compartment would generally encounter "a pretty frosty reception."

Exceptions were made. Bede Loneragan continues: "Christmas and Easter were the big celebratory times. There were a lot of public servants travelling on the train in those days, and the public servants used to make it their business to be early and they would decorate the whole of the train externally. They'd start at the engine and they'd festoon the front of the engine and both sides of it with streamers and balloons. At Central Station. Never in the morning, always coming home at night ... you don't feel like celebrating at seven o'clock in the morning.

"The fireman and the driver of the trains used to get in the act and they'd put their party hats on and they'd have balloons, streamers, oh all sorts of things, anything they could lay their hands on, to decorate the train. Christmas and Easter were really slap-up parties and they would go on from the time we left Central until the time we got off the train. The whole train became involved. After you'd gone through Strathfield I doubt very much if half the train knew where their seats were ..."

"When I look back over it", concludes Alan Lewis, "the old 'steamed fish' trains really had character, you know. This great big engine with all the power bottled up inside it. It was really something and part of the life of the Mountains."

The last run of The Fish up the Mountains on 4 March, 1957. (State Rail Authority)

"When the Visitors Go"
by Henry Lawson

At the end of 1921, following a spell in hospital, Henry Lawson was sent by friends to the Blue Mountains in the hope that the clean mountain air would revive his failing health. Lawson spent Christmas and New Year "resuscitating on the Hills" and the local newspaper, the *Blue Mountains Echo,* noted his visit in its issue of 6 January, 1922. "He is no new chum to Katoomba", it reported. "He knew it nearly 40 years ago and in a chat with Harry Peckman, the Mountain poet of the early days, many memories long dead were revived." 'When the Visitors Go', "a few random verses" penned during his stay, was published in the same issue. Eight months later Lawson was dead. (*Photo courtesy John Low*)

"When the time is close and the train is near ..." from When the Visitors Go
(ca. 1930, State Rail Authority)

We all were "permanent" long ago,
When Christmas came with a hint of snow,
We worked on buildings and lived in a tent;
But we always were dull when the visitors went.

The lady tourist in days agone
Had cap and jacket and knickers on;
Her mate was somewhat similar, too,
With legs of yellow and wings of blue.

And when we saw 'em we'd always run
Like sheol, to the camp to get our gun.
We'd shout: "You mightn't see 'em agen!"
Such birds were rare on the Mountain then.

We all were young, with our tools for pens;
And we called the visitors "Specimens" —
All this is childish and weak I know —
But this is a song when the visitors go.

Above, first four stanzas When the Visitors Go *Blue Mountains Echo, 6 January 1922*

A Select Bibliography

ASTON, Nell, *Rails, Roads and Ridges: History of Lapstone Hill — Glenbrook*, Glenbrook Public School Centenary Committee, 1988.

BAKER, M. & CORRINGHAM, R., *Birds of the Blue Mountains*, Winmalee, Three Sisters, 1988.

BAKER, Margaret et. al., *Native Plants of the Lower Blue Mountains*, Winmalee, Three Sisters, 1985.

BAKER, Margaret et. al., *Native plants of the Upper Blue Mountains*, Winmalee, Three Sisters, 1984.

BAYLEY, William A., *Lapstone Zig Zag Railway*, Bulli, Austrail, 1975.

BAYLEY, William A. *The Great Zig Zag Railway at Lithgow*, Bulli, Austrail, 1977.

BATES, Geoff, *The Carrington Hotel*, Blackheath, The Author, 1982.

BECHERVAISE, John, *Blue Mountains Sketchbook*, Adelaide, Rigby, 1971.

BELBIN, P. & BURKE, D., *Full Steam Across the Mountains*, North Ryde, Methuen, 1981.

BENTLEY, James, *Black Smoke, Blue Mountains: The Great Zig Zag Railway*, Bathurst, Robert Brown, 1988.

BENTLEY, S.J., *'Christmas Swamp': A History of Lawson*, Springwood Historical Society, 1986.

CAMPBELL, Mary et. al., *Hazelbrook Heritage: A Social History of Hazelbrook and Woodford*, Hazelbrook Public School Parents & Citizens Association, 1989.

DUNKLEY, John R., *Jenolan Caves as they were in the Nineteenth Century*, Sydney, Speleological Research Council, 1986.

HUNGERFORD, M. & DONALD, J., *Exploring the Blue Mountains*, Kenthurst, Kangaroo Press, 1982.

KAY, Phillip, *The Far-Famed Blue Mountains of Harry Phillips*, Leura, Second Back Row Press, 1985.

LIDDLE, David, *Blue Mountains Wilderness*, Leura, Second Back Row Press, 1987.

MACKANESS, George ed., *Fourteen Journeys Over the Blue Mountains of New South Wales, 1813-1841*, Sydney, Horwitz-Grahame, 1965.

MOSLEY, Geoff, *Blue Mountains for World Heritage*, Sydney, Colong Foundation for Wilderness, 1989.

O'CONNOR, Mark, *Poetry of the Mountains*, Leura, Second Back Row Press, 1988.

POWELL, Greg, *Bushwalking Through History — The Blue Mountains*, Hampton, Vic., Macstyle, 1989.

RALSTON, Basil, *Jenolan: The Golden Ages of Caving*, Winmalee, Three Sisters, 1989.

RICHMOND, Coralie, *Blue Mountains, The City Within a Park*, The Author, 1987.

ROTARY CLUB OF BLACKHEATH, *Historic Blackheath*, 1977.

ROTARY CLUB OF KATOOMBA, *Old Leura and Katoomba*, 1982.

SEARLE, Alan, *Places of Historic Interest on the Lower Blue Mountains*, Springwood Hist. Society, 1977.

SEARLE, Alan, *The History of Faulconbridge, Linden and Woodford*, Springwood Hist. Society 1986.

SMITH, Jim, *The Blue Mountains Mystery Track: Lindeman Pass*, Winmalee, Three Sisters, 1990.

SMITH, Jim, *From Katoomba to Jenolan Caves: The Six Foot Track, 1884-1984*, Katoomba, Second Back Row Press, 1984.

SMITH, Jim, *How to See the Blue Mountains*, (2nd ed.), Katoomba, Second Back Row Press, 1986.

SMITH, Jim, *What is Happening to the Blue Mountains?* Katoomba, Second Back Row Press, 1981.

SMITH, Judy & Peter, *Fauna of the Blue Mountains*, Kenthurst, Kangaroo Press, 1990.

SPEIRS, Hugh, *Landscape Art and the Blue Mountains*, Chippendale, APCOL, 1981.

STEWART, Douglas, *Norman Lindsay: A Personal Memoir*, Melbourne, Nelson, 1975.

STANBURY, Peter ed., *The Blue Mountains, Grand Adventure for All*, (2nd ed.), Leura, Second Back Row Press, 1988.

SMOLICZ, R. & LOW, J., *Historic Blue Mountains*, Katoomba, Blue Mountains City Council, 1987.

WATKINS, Paul, *A Portrait of the City of Blue Mountains*, Bathurst, Robert Brown, 1988.

WILEY, Rebecca, *A Visit to Norman Lindsay at Springwood, May 1918*, Sydney, Angus & Robertson, 1986.

Of the three historical societies operating in the Blue Mountains the oldest is the **Blue Mountains Historical Society** formed in 1946. It holds general meetings once a

Of the three historical societies operating in the Blue Mountains the oldest is the **Blue Mountains Historical Society** formed in 1946. It holds general meetings once a month and has a very active research group that also meets monthly. Historic trips, are part of its programme. The Society also runs the Hobby's Reach Museum at Wentworth Falls and has a growing collection of books, photographs, etc. Its address is P.O. Box 17, Wentworth Falls 2782.

Springwood Historical Society was established in 1955 (originally as the Macquarie Historical Society). It meets monthly, organises historical bus tours and publishes a quarterly bulletin as well as the occasional monograph. The Society does not run a museum but its large collection of photographs, books and papers has been organised and indexed at the Springwood Library by an enthusiastic group of society members. It operates as an independent collection under the supervision of the Local Studies Librarian. The Society's address is P.O. Box 387, Springwood 2777.

The **Mount Victoria & District Historical Society** began life as the Mount York Historical Society in 1965. It meets monthly and operates a large museum in the old Refreshment Rooms of Mount Victoria Railway Station. The Society also publishes the occasional monograph on aspects of the district's history. Its address is C/- 45 Bathurst Rd., Mount Victoria 2786.

The **Blue Mountains City Library's Local Studies Collection** was begun in 1982. It is housed in 'Braemar' attached to Springwood Library and is accessible by appointment. The collection includes books, photographs, pamphlet material, newspapers, maps, oral history recordings and archives of local government, individuals and community organisations. Enquiries should be directed to the Local Studies Librarian, Blue Mountains City Library, Macquarie Rd., Springwood 2777.

The **Blue Mountains Family History Society** was formed in 1986. It meets monthly at Springwood Library where it also runs regular workshops. The Society publishes a magazine, *The Explorers Tree*, four times a year and has embarked upon a major project to transcribe all the Blue Mountains cemeteries and publish the information with biographical details where available. Two volumes have already been published. The Society's address is P.O. Box 97, Springwood 2777.

CHRONOLOGY

22,240 ± 1,000 Before Present:: Human occupation of Kings Tableland, Wentworth Falls.

12,500 ± 145 Before Present:: Human occupation of Lyre Bird Dell, Leura.

12,000 ± 350 Before Present:: Human occupation of Walls Cave, Blackheath.

1788: Governor Phillip sights the Blue Mountains for the first time from a point north of present-day Pennant Hills.

1789: Captain Watkin Tench discovers the Nepean River.
Lt. William Dawes crosses the Nepean and succeeds in reaching a point north-west of Faulconbridge-Linden.

1793: Captain William Paterson explores the Grose River.

1794: Henry Hacking claims to have penetrated 32 kilometres further inland than any other European. His route is unknown.

1795: Matthew Everingham's expedition explores the northern Blue Mountains reaching, possibly, Mount Irvine or Mount Tomah.

1796: George Bass ventures into the lower Burragorang Valley almost reaching Kanangra Walls.

1798: John Wilson leads a party into the mountains south-west of Sydney.

1802: Ensign Francis Barrallier heads west from the Wollondilly River almost reaching the Kanangra Plateau.

1804: George Caley reaches Mount Banks (now Mount King George) in the northern Blue Mountains.

1807: David Dickinson Mann leads an expedition into the Blue Mountains. His route is unknown.

1813: The expedition of Gregory Blaxland, William Lawson and William Charles Wentworth is successful in finding a route across the Blue Mountains.

1814: George Evans completes a survey of the Blaxland, Lawson & Wentworth route and pushes about 160 kilometres further west.

1815: A convict road party under the supervision of William Cox completes a road to the site of Bathurst.
Governor Lachlan Macquarie and his entourage travel over the new road and proclaim the site of Bathurst. The Governor also names Springwood and Blackheath.

1816: The military depot established the previous year at Glenbrook Lagoon is moved to Springwood.

1819: Quoy, Gaudichaud and Pellion, three members of a French scientific expedition, travel over the Blue Mountains.

1822: Mrs Elizabeth Hawkins and her family travel to Bathurst.
Barron Field travels to Bathurst.

1823: Lawson's Long Alley is constructed down the western escarpment as an alternative to Cox's route.
James McBrien resurveys the line of the Western Road.
Archibald Bell discovers a new route to the west via Kurrajong.

The Golden Fleece (Collits' Inn) opened at the foot of Mount York.

1824: Lawson's Zig Zag road (now Old Bathurst Road) replaces Cox's road as the principal route up the eastern escarpment.

ca. 1827: The Weatherboard Inn opens (Wentworth Falls).

1828: Major Thomas L. Mitchell becomes Surveyor-General on the death of John Oxley.
Construction of an alternative descent at Mount York begins under the supervision of Major E. Lockyer. It is later abandoned when Mitchell transfers operations to the Victoria Pass.

1830: The Pilgrim Inn, built in the late 1820s, receives its first licence.

1831: The Valley Inn (later The Woolpack and The Welcome Inn) opens at Valley Heights.
The Scotch Thistle (Gardner's Inn) opens at Blackheath.

1832: David Lennox arrives in Australia and is employed by Mitchell to construct a bridge on the new Pass at Lapstone Hill.
Victoria Pass opened by Governor Bourke.

1833: Lennox Bridge at Lapstone is completed.

1834: Mitchell's Pass up Lapstone Hill is opened.
First grant of land at Springwood given to William Lawson.

1835: The Quaker, James Backhouse, travels over the Blue Mountains.

1836: Charles Darwin travels to Bathurst, stopping at The Weatherboard and Blackheath.

1839: Louisa Meredith travels over the Blue Mountains, spending a night at The Shepherd and His Flock Inn (Blind Paddy's) at Pulpit Hill.
The Mount Victoria Inn is opened at the foot of Victoria Pass.

1840: The Blue Mountain Inn opened at Lawson.

1844: The military stockade at Bull's Camp moves to Blackheath.

1845: The Springwood Inn (Boland's Inn) opened at Springwood.

1846: Lt. Colonel Godfrey Charles Mundy travels over the Blue Mountains to Bathurst with Governor Fitzroy.

1849: Toll Bars established at Seventeen Mile Hollow (Linden) and Broughton's Waterhole (Mount Victoria).
The Blackheath Stockade is closed. Replaced by a Mounted Police Station and Lock-up.

1851: Gold discovered at Ophir.

1856: John Whitton is appointed Engineer-in-chief of the N.S.W. Railways.

1863: The Welcome Inn at Mount Victoria opens.

1865: Sir Frederick Pottinger is accidentally shot at the Pilgrim Inn while on his way to Sydney.

1866: The Binda or Fish River Caves (Jenolan adopted in 1884) Reserve is created by the N.S.W. Government.

1867: The Western Railway line is opened to The Weatherboard (Wentworth Falls).
Jeremiah Wilson is appointed 'Keeper of the Caves'. He holds office until 1896.

1868: The Western Railway line reaches Mount Victoria.
H.R.H. Prince Alfred, Duke of Edinburgh, travels by train to The Weatherboard and picnics at the Falls.

1869: The Western Railway line is opened to Bowenfels after the completion of The Great Zig Zag.

1871: St Peter's Anglican Church, Mt Victoria, is built. The oldest church still standing in the Blue Mountains.

1874: An astronomical station is established at Woodford to observe the Transit of Venus.

1875: Frederick Eccleston Du Faur purchases land at Mount Wilson and establishes his artists' camp in the Grose Valley.

1876: Charles Moore builds his country residence, Moorecourt, at Springwood.
Balmoral guesthouse opens in Katoomba.

1877: Sir Henry Parkes moves to Faulconbridge.

1878: John Britty North registers his Katoomba Coal Mine.
Three crew are killed in a head-on train collision at the foot of Lapstone Hill.
Springwood Public School opens.

1879: The Tarana-Fish River Caves Road is completed.
The Blue Mountain railway station (opened in 1867) now known as Lawson.
Wascoe's becomes Blaxland.

1880: Jeremiah Wilson erects the first accommodation house at the Caves.

1881: H.R.H. Prince Albert and Prince George visit the Blue Mountains and enjoy breakfast with Sir Henry and Lady Parkes at Faulconbridge.

1882: The Great Western Hotel (later The Carrington) is opened in Katoomba.
Katoomba Public School opens.

1884: The Six-Foot Bridle Track from Katoomba to Jenolan Caves is opened.
A wall and fence is built around the Explorers' Tree at Katoomba, resulting eventually in its death.
John Fletcher opens the Katoomba College.

1885: J.B. North forms a second mining company at Katoomba, The Katoomba Coal and Shale Company.
The villages of Glenbrook and Blackheath are proclaimed.

1889: Peckman Brothers begin the first daily coach service from Katoomba to Jenolan Caves.
Katoomba is gazetted a Municipality.
'Lilianfels', the country home of Sir Frederick and Lady Darley, is built in Katoomba.

1890: The first Katoomba Municipal Council is elected.
The Australian Kerosene Oil & Mineral Company takes

over J.B. North's activities at the Ruined Castle and Orphan Rock.
1891: Arthur Streeton paints "Fires On" at Lapstone Hill.
1892: The Mount Victoria Inn is bought by J.W. Berghofer as a private residence and renamed 'Rosentha'l (later changed to 'Rosedale').
James Hunter Lawson builds both the Oriental Hotel and 'Braemar' in Springwood.
The Lapstone Zig Zag is replaced by a tunnel through Lapstone Hill.
1896: F.J. Wilson is appointed caretaker of Jenolan Caves. He holds office until 1903.
Sir Henry Parkes dies and is buried at Faulconbridge.
1897: Springwood Ladies College is established in Moorecourt at Springwood.
Katoomba Courthouse opens.
1901: The Duchess of York (later Queen Mary) visits Katoomba and enjoys afternoon tea at 'Lilianfels'.
1903: J.C. 'Voss' Wiburd becomes Caretaker at Jenolan Caves. He holds office until 1932.
1904: The Hydro Majestic opens as a hydropathic sanatorium at Medlow Bath.
1905: The Katoomba & Leura Tourist Association is formed.
1906: The Kanimbla Shire Council is established.
1907: The Kanimbla Shire Council changes its name to The Blue Mountains Shire Council.
Katoomba Waterworks is opened by Governor Sir Harry Rawson.
Woodford Academy opens under headmaster John Frazer McManamey.
1908: Harry Phillips (photographer) arrives in Katoomba.
Stratford Girls School moves into 'The Palace' (built 1870s) guesthouse at Lawson.
1910: The Great Zig Zag at Lithgow is replaced by a system of ten tunnels.
1912: Norman and Rose Lindsay purchase Maryville at Faulconbridge.
The Lord Byron Inn (built ca. 1837) at Blaxland is demolished.
Berghofer's Pass is opened as a motoring alternative to the steep Victoria Pass.
1913: The new railway route up the eastern escarpment, replacing the deviation opened in 1892, is now in full operation.
St George's Anglican Church at Mount Wilson is consecrated.
Electric power for Katoomba is generated from The Carrington Hotel.
1915: The Coo-ee recruitment march passes through the Blue Mountains.
1918: The four-storey section of Jenolan Caves House is completed.

1919: Blackheath is proclaimed a Municipality.
1920: H.R.H. Edward, Prince of Wales, visits the Blue Mountains, stopping at Lawson.
1923: The Osborne Ladies College moves to Blackheath from the Sydney suburb of Epping.
1925: A local syndicate in Katoomba forms the Katoomba Colliery Ltd. and re-opens J.B. North's old mine at South Katoomba. Power generation for Katoomba and surrounding area comes under local government control.
1926: The Blue Mountains District Ambulance Service is established.
The Great Western Highway from Emu Plains to Blaxland opened along the route of the old railway line.
1927: The Duke and Duchess of York visit the Blue Mountains.
1928: Poet and editor David McKee Wright dies at Glenbrook.
1931: Don Bradman hits a century in three overs at Blackheath.
The Dog Face Rock at Katoomba collapses forming 'The Landslide'.
1932: The Giant Stairway and Projecting Platform Lookout at Echo Point are officially opened by the Hon. B.S.B. Stevens, Premier of N.S.W.
1933: The Katoomba Colliery Scenic Electric Cable Railway is officially launched.
1934: The Duke of Gloucester stops briefly at Katoomba Railway Station.
Hinkler Park opened in Katoomba.
1936: The Kings Theatre in Katoomba is demolished and replaced by The Savoy.
1937: The Wyoming guesthouse (formerly the Woolpack Inn) at Valley Heights is demolished.
The Empire Theatre at Katoomba undergoes extensive renovation and re-opens as The Embassy.
1938: The original Scotch Thistle at Blackheath is demolished.
1946: The Municipality of Katoomba is proclaimed a City.
1947: The City of Blue Mountains is formed through an amalgamation of the Shire of Blue Mountains, the City of Katoomba and the Municipality of Blackheath.
1954: Queen Elizabeth II visits the Blue Mountains.
1957: The Scenic Skyway is opened.
Bushfires devastate the township of Leura.
1964: Poet Zora Cross dies at Glenbrook.
1968: The Pilgrim Inn at Blaxland is destroyed by bushfire.
1969: Norman Lindsay dies at Springwood.
1972: North Springwood officially becomes Winmalee.
1973: The Norman Lindsay Gallery and Museum is officially opened at Faulconbridge.
1985: Novelist Eleanor Dark dies in Katoomba.
1987: Artist George Finey dies at Lawson.
1988: Novelist and Blackheath resident Kylie Tennant dies.

Available at all good bookshops and newsagents. If unavailable please phone (02) 9439–5093.

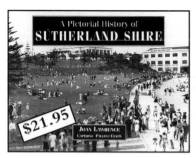
A Pictorial History of SUTHERLAND SHIRE — JOAN LAWRENCE, CAPTIONS: PAULINE CURBY — $21.95

A Pictorial History of CRONULLA — PAULINE CURBY — $21.95

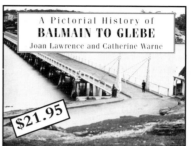
Pictorial Memories ST GEORGE, Rockdale, Kogarah, Hurstville — Joan Lawrence — $21.95

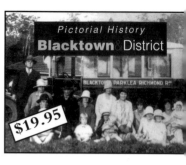
A Pictorial History of BALMAIN TO GLEBE — Joan Lawrence and Catherine Warne — $21.95

Pictorial History Blacktown & District — $19.95

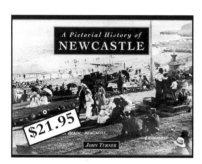
A Pictorial History of NEWCASTLE — JOHN TURNER — $21.95

PICTORIAL HISTORY EASTERN SUBURBS — Edited by Joan Lawrence and Alan Sharpe — $21.95

A Pictorial History of Canterbury Bankstown — Joan Lawrence, Brian Madden and Leslie Muir — $21.95

Pictorial Memories Manly to Palm Beach — $21.95

PICTORIAL HISTORY Lavender Bay to The Spit — BLUES POINT • LAVENDER BAY • MCMAHONS POINT • KIRRIBILLI • NEUTRAL BAY • CREMORNE • CLIFTON GARDENS • BALMORAL • MOSMAN • THE SPIT • BEAUTY POINT — JOAN LAWRENCE — $24.95

PICTORIAL HISTORY NEWTOWN — ALEXANDRIA • CAMPERDOWN • DARLINGTON • ERSKINEVILLE • MACDONALDTOWN • ST PETERS • WATERLOO — ALAN SHARPE — $24.95

PICTORIAL HISTORY City of Sydney — ALAN SHARPE — $24.95

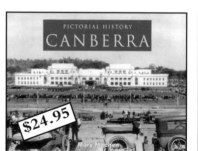
PICTORIAL HISTORY CANBERRA — Mary Mitchem — $24.95

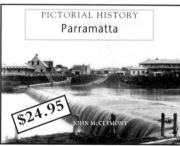
PICTORIAL HISTORY Parramatta — JOHN McCLYMONT — $24.95

Forthcoming titles: Randwick, Penrith, Hawkesbury and Bega Valley Shire.

Kingsclear Books PO Box 335, Alexandria 1435.
Email kingsclear@wr.com.au / www.kingsclearbooks.com.au